AF261833

CONTEMPORARY POLITIC

CONTEMPORARY POLITIC

A Guide to the Structures Behind Modern Politics

Baruch Menache

Contents:

PART I: WHAT MAKES SOMETHING POLITICAL: A STRUCTURAL INQUIRY 1

Chapter One: Contention, Violence, and the Boundaries of the Political 1

Chapter Two: Metaphor as the Basis for Political Conceptualization 5

Chapter Three: Personalization, Enlargement, and the Danger of Metaphor 11

Chapter Four: Simulation vs. Metaphor vs. Domestication 21

Chapter Five: The Embodiment of the Political Strata 33

Part II: Three Pillars of the Politic: Structure, Sequence, and the Political 37

Chapter One: Three Beliefs to Maintain a Civilized Structure 39

The Structural Belief: Foundations of Civilization and Consciousness 39

Second Belief: The Role of Political Structure in Maintaining Universal and Sequential Order 41

Third Belief: The Political Sequential organization and Its Role in Stabilizing Infrastructure and Universal Order 43

Sequential Synergy: Structure, Politics, and the Natural Order 49

Part III: Institutional Structures 61

Chapter One: Institutions, Consciousness, and the Architecture of Exchange 63

Chapter Two: Political Institutions and Constitutions 73

Chapter Three: Educational Institutions 79

The Two Types of Schooling: Contextual Learning vs. Consciousness Interaction 85

Chapter Four: The Dynamics of Hierarchical Exchange and Social Evolution 87

Hierarchy, System Participation, and the Loss of Contrast 88

Part IV: Law, Evidence and Justice 91

Chapter One: Law, Sociality, and the Limits of Political Direction 93

Chapter Two: The Charitable Balance of Private and Public Law 103

Chapter Three: The Ownership Ideal: Between Interaction and Political Proclamation 105

The Dynamics of Ownership 109

Chapter Four: Evidential and Non-Evidential: A Dual Framework of Reality 113

Chapter Five: Three Layers of Truth: On Psyche, Structure, and Evidentiary Reality 115

Part V: Politics and Consciousness 123

Chapter One: The Encapsulation of Consciousness: A Reflection on Historical Vantage Points 125

The Encapsulation of Consciousness in a High-Conscious Environment 128

Chapter Three: The Role of Domestication in Conscious Processing 131

Chapter Four: The Detrimental Effects of Encapsulating Consciousness 133

Part VI: From Political Theory to Practice; Symbols, Stories & Systemic Response 143

Chapter One: The Symbolic Hierarchy of Aesthetic Prowess and Class Structure 145

Chapter Two: The Illusion of Biological Continuity in Global Political Constructs 147

Chapter Three: Secondary Narratives and the Conflict of Resolution 155

Chapter Four: The Constructs of Existential Risk: Individual, Institutional, and Conceptual Domains 161

Chapter Five: Real-Time Evolution and Collective Cognition 165

Chapter Six: The Decline of Civilization 175

PART I: WHAT MAKES SOMETHING POLITICAL: A STRUCTURAL INQUIRY

Chapter One: Contention, Violence, and the Boundaries of the Political

We will always find certain characteristics in the political realm which will assist in narrowing down the search for its realistic nature. Firstly, the political will always be contentious, with varying degrees of this characteristic. The contentiousness is not a negative trait but rather a manifestation of the normal workings of the political realm. Social investment into the area of the political realm will always be present, and what is not cared for by the people will not be political due to its distance from the center.

However, not every contentious idea is political. For instance, parenting is a contentious idea that will bring strong emotion for most in engagement with it, yet it may not be considered political. The reason that it is contentious is that all of humanity has an emotional bond to parenting, in terms of their own memory of being parented, or how they have attempted to mirror that in their own lives. The contentiousness arises due to the depth of intimacy related to the ideas being brought forth.

The reason that a contentious idea does not become political is because there is no intersection between the *idea* and a governing body. Parenting tactics, unless facing extremes which would have a governing body involve itself, do not intersect with the political realm. Sexuality, for instance, does not necessarily intersect with a governing body.

A parade or demonstration about certain issues can either be turned into being considered political or can be separated from it. The act of demonstration is to highlight a specific issue to the institutions of power or governing bodies. When that demonstration is specifically existent to raise awareness without a clear intersection with a governing body, we will not call it political. A religious demonstration, which is only attempting to bring awareness to the public of their ideas, is not political. This is true only when we cannot envision a possible intersection into the established governing bodies.

When there is an act of burning something at a demonstration, it would be considered political. The intersection is not as clear, yet the *act* of violence in a public burning is also a demand of all governing bodies to care for this issue, or "there will be more violence." Had the demonstration occurred without the burning ceremony, we may not call it political, since it is only an awareness campaign.

Acts of violence will be political as long as the governing bodies are interested in preventing them from manifesting into the public arena. Domestic violence, for instance, is not necessarily political, due to the fact that the governing bodies are less interested in its nature and will not be a major intersection.

We find that there is a parallel between the governing body and its interest in public issues as opposed to private issues. The reason being is that the governing body is a representation of the people in an institutionalized form. The act of public burning is a public issue but is also one which the governing body is concerned about. The availability for a slight act of violence automatically threatens the existence of the governing body, since it would lose the ability to govern. When there is availability of violence in its streets, any aspect of governing would sense vulnerability, since it cannot prevent the chief among them: the prevention of violence.

Yet there can be an existent governing body while anarchy reigns amongst the populace, either to be against the violence or to be disassociated from it. Had the governing body cared for a matter which was of no interest to the anarchist, they could work side by side. The political aspects would be limited to that which intersects with the governing body. For instance, if the governing body is an institution for mediating health norms amongst the populace, and the anarchists are aligned with such a system. Even if law was lawless and violence was the norm, this institution of health would exist alongside that. When a health matter arises, it will become political due to its intersection with that governing body. This is hard to imagine, since with a lack of stability, professional institutions are unable to govern with much freedom or progress.

In anarchist rule, acts of violence are not political insofar as they do not intersect with any governing body which attempts to prove even more violent. The revolutionary measure of violence will not dent the political realm, for there is none to receive them. The only option to ascertain a political statement is to defend violence, and in doing so become a governing body over violent acts. Only then will acts of violence return to the spotlight of the political world, for there is an institution that is wary of its movements. Therefore, the beginning stages of a governing body can be found as a defense against violence, which is the establishment of governing violence.

This governing body must be institutionalized in a manner that is agreeable as such by the majority of the public. We could imagine a tribunal of an ethnic group, which seems like a governing body, but because it is active in a vacuum away from the public's agreement that such stands as an institution, it does not become political. The governing body must be that which is associated as such throughout the populace, and if that legitimacy is questioned, so will the sentiment of *the political* weaken

Chapter Two: Metaphor as the Basis for Political Conceptualization

There is a prevalence of a sort of national entity because the political structure is the oversight of all other systems. There is nothing higher than that, and the oligarchic or cooperative systems are only dependent on the primary political structure. They retain a sort of premise that follows their own parameters but remain under the political system, while the political sphere includes them as but a single part of all other systems. This can sometimes be misconstrued as the primary reality structure instead of genuine actualization, owed to this premise of regulating all other systems. We presume, because it acts like any other system, it is an agent like all others, but in reality, there is no agent nor agency.

The only reason that a political structure exists at all is because a sociality permeates that existence. We could say that at any given time, political structures fade into oblivion for their lack of social agreement, and others are constructed due to their social stimulation. Not all systems are reliant on sociality, for instance, a neighborhood, city, or other geographical establishment. These are both reliant on sociality and concrete elements. There is a border between houses, neighborhoods, and cities, and this border does not act as a border but rather as the existential experience of individuals. One gains a sense of the border of their abode because of both the external sensibilities that claim external ground and because one can only "download" their abode to a particular direction and limitation.

The same can be said for residents of a city, where each negotiates their abodement and such settlement of their ownership of the city. A country or political organization does not retain individual residence because it is a conceptual organization that usurps other systems but does not possess personalization. Even if one were to reside on its border, they would not experience a personal sentiment toward the border, as there is no natural negotiation; only the enforcement of the political structure. The neighborhood, town, city, and other infrastructures built from multitudes of individuations are negotiated daily as to what constitutes externalities and their degree of externality.

The change of season could have a city move from one location to another, afforded by the individuals who take up an abodement to constitute the existential experience of the city. The topic of how that occurs is for another occasion.

Therefore, the major cities of a political system are always in conflict with the political system, because on one side is an existential abodement of individuals and their biological experiences, and the other is a system that does not relate to the individual yet retains oversight of the city. Until the institution of a political entity, there is only the city, which is regulated not by consideration of a constitution or effective governance but by its internal sociality. Similar to how a neighborhood of some moral standing can govern itself without the need of external parties; based on biological necessity, willing negotiation, and all the social exchanges necessary for righteous dealings.

When the city moves beyond that process, it resembles what is very similar to a stock exchange, a mirror city that overlays the real city, and exchanges and governs from that simulation. This simulation has enough connections to the real arena that it is taken seriously by all. When the stock loses its value, it is either recalibrating with the real entity or revealing that the connection between the simulation and the real entity is severed.

The political entity acts in the same manner: it follows the circumstances of the "neighborhood" but does so from the vantage of a conceptual landscape, mirroring the processes which occur beneath its rubric. The individual can never truly connect with the political process of the city or neighborhood, but can reside and abode in the realm, revealing a certain social experience that parallels others yet remains deeply personal and ever-changing.

We must notice when a social dialogue discusses a neighborhood, city, or state from the standpoint of *abodement*; where biological circumstances are negotiated to differentiate this from discussions rooted in market illustrations. The issue is apparent in market discourse, where even the language mirrors that of real entities. The real market is a social infrastructure for the exchange of goods within a geographical locale, whereas the financial market is a simulation of that reality.

When an entity is described as "valuable," it represents a simulation of its value, not an internal valuation. This is difficult to calculate, as such value might include unquantifiable amenities that cannot be liquidized or recognized. Thus, an avid market reader must follow both the simulated value as well as the entity itself, since there may be discord between public interest and internal reality.

Anyone who dwells in a real entity in relation to its market perception cannot fully reflect the simulation of their establishment, not due to excessive knowledge, but because of their biological attachment that cannot be reflected upon. They are experiencing the internal system and cannot take a detached view of its simulation. Even if they attempt such, they will only to fail at properly understanding its realm due to their existential attachment. Those in the market exchange recognize not to be existentially involved in ventures, as this would cause an abundance of information, losing the simulating character, creating a blend that causes fault in both categories.

This is why someone who dwells in the city can never discuss the city, or they could, but it would be improper information, as they are recording a milieu of sociality that does not concern the thing itself but rather its simulation. Only the political oversight of the city can view it from that vantage and make judgments, just as the analyst speculates about organizations.

This is most true for the state's political structure, which has the furthermost oversight and thus is the most simulated compared to the real entity it claims to govern. Within this simulation of political conceptualization, there is still a certain gain from personal attachment. While there is no direct mirror to the real entity on the ground (for at least the city's political entity simulates the real city), the political entity of a state does not have a "real state" for the ground; it is made up of real entities, simulations, and other systems, all bundled into what is called the political entity.

If the political edifice is embedded in market exchange, there is no way to derive a result from the perspective of its systems, because they are not tangible when bundled together, only when separate, and even then, only within their respective simulations. The political entity's attachment to its sub-entities relies on a social agreement to its conceptualization. While a city's political overlay may depend on social agreement, it does not require it to the same degree as individuals' dwelling and existential attachment vitalize its system.

The political conceptualization lacks personal existential attachment because there is no dwelling within a state; only based on a conglomerate of sociality. For this reason, the simulated attachment to the political conceptualization, without existential attachment, becomes dependent on the social agreement of its structure. Since individuals do not existentially partake in the state, their agreement is weak; there is no fundamental reason for the connection. Of course, they may desire peace and stability, but that desire is existentially relevant only in their local context, not throughout the broader conceptualization of a vast political system.

Therefore, the volatility of a state as a concept means that the agreement of sociality is based on the attachment from individual to the state. Considering that this attachment is fragile due to a lack of existential viability, the individual must generate sentiment to maintain that instance. How they do this is of paramount importance and constitutes the definition of the actualization of a state. If they presume a personalization of the state, they are merely imagining a conceptualization for the purpose of connection; providing social agreement not to the state's true nature, but to an imagined personalization. This is a projection of how they would like to view the state to regulate and control their stance.

We have already entertained the representativeness of the political system, functioning as a metaphor for the regulation of parental figures and godlike entities. It is treated as the forebear of consciousness and all individualistic potential. This metaphor is the manner through which most individuals engineer a connection, because it must appear as a form of oversight, encompassing all systems, and thus takes the grandeur of parental or divine figures. When the metaphor is more sophisticated, it can represent consciousness and individual potential, or alternatively, systemic organization or other conceptualization that engenders the metaphor.

Most individuals will adopt a metaphor performed as a reality structure, or something akin to it, allowing them to interact with reality as if it were a substantiated structure. However, this remains merely as a metaphor, for we have agreed that the political entity is least substantial in existential reality, and thus requires these mental feats to allow a sociality that would have it appear as a conceptualized reality.

Because of its metaphorical standing, any attempt to bridge the metaphor to the real thing becomes troublesome for the psyche in addition to sociality. Irony, when bridged, does not produce the same effect, but rather reverses its clause to such a degree that it appears as its opposite. The ironic form of "black" which is assumed to be real must become as white as possible in order to remain relatable to black and still function as irony, thus allowing white to be considered genuine, all the while remaining ironic because it is true that through white, black is revealed via ironic formation. Metaphor, on the other hand, does not work in the same way; it parallels the real thing via an illusion and imitative realm that is more relatable to individuality.

If we take the metaphor too seriously, we risk mistaking the imitative realm for reality, one which does not allow for a through line to the real thing, as it focuses solely on a realm that presumes to exist. Metaphor retains its vitality even when it comes too close for parallel processing because its connection to reality does not depend on the real thing itself.

Differing from irony, which lacks a basis of its identifiable nature to vitalize, metaphor possesses a unique system that works irrespective of the realm it attempts to illustrate. We would not approach a metaphorical realm at the onset if we assumed it to be the only reality as it is fairly fragile in its own connection to reality. The fairy tale would not be enjoined if it were assumed to be the only reality, even as it does possess a unique connection to reality: imagery that individuals experience, relational material that mirrors one's own, and other such themes, which are not metaphors but reflections of reality that offer vitality to the fairy tale realm.

However, we do not simply enter those realms because of this stranded attachment; we do so because they promise a metaphorical aspect that illustrates something real. This is the natural process of a child, or adult, in their approach to these realms: they enter only upon the promise of metaphorical value. The same applies to the political realm. If one were to trace their history of attachment to that conceptualization, they would notice that it only became relevant because it promised a certain "entertainment" value, or more accurately, a metaphorical value to gain access to something real.

Chapter Three: Personalization, Enlargement, and the Danger of Metaphor

Only later, upon forgetting that initial process, does the fairy tale or political structure begin to take on the assumption of a realm that is true to itself. Of course, the fairy tale does not gain that presumption as readily as the political formation, because it contains fewer attachments to individual reality. However, the political realm can only be assumed as a premise because of what it promises to retain as a metaphor. While it is an offering of a metaphor, it becomes wearisome when it continuously assumes the role of reality rather than the real thing to which it initially pointed.[i]

The same is true of markets, in the experience of proper exchange, the individual would never assume the market to be the quintessential reality but rather a way of perceiving another reality. With that in mind, one would be able to sequence trades with awareness of the system's workings. But when perceived as reality, it becomes 'finances in one's pocket', with all its immediate associations, rather than a conceptual structure that reflects the reality of finances without fully inhabiting it.

We begin to approach the distinction between metaphor and reality itself. We could postulate that metaphor can be found in relational material because it always directs toward a preliminary state; which can be considered the real aspect. The current family body could be a metaphor for the childhood family body, and the childhood family body, a metaphor for individual potential.

However, we will define and distinguish metaphor as that which is not constructed to simulate a reality framework, but always to serve the real thing. The current family body serves its own construction, even as it alludes to psychic parts that are more existent. Anything that functions as its own reality structure should not be considered a metaphor, as it establishes its own ground and warrants independent study, apart from any reference to something more real or tangible.

Metaphor enables language, and essentially, experience, to do what is possible with feeling, but not with reality. If one wants to engage with a city, the only possible way to do so may be to construct a metaphorical reality that constitutes a city concept to offer as a point of reference for sensibilities; and thus, feelings. These feelings cannot emerge if one engages with the city in real time and embodied experience, because it consists of individuals, habitats, and constructed systems, but not an all-inclusive "city" that invokes sensibilities or personal feelings. There is no reservoir of personalization in the entirety of a city; it is made possible only through a metaphorical perspective.

This differs from personalization, for example, when one personalizes the sky as 'heavens.' While this is a metaphor, it is more an attempt to place self into the object; an attempt to integrate that object into one's existential state. Heaven becomes a metaphorical reference to something beyond, but it is also used in a deeply personal sense; between individual and object.

We might say one person personalizes the object, while another experiences such metaphorically. A spiritual leader might view the sky as metaphorically imbued with meaning, while a creative or emotional individual might see the sky as an extension of their inner sensibility projected onto the landscape.

Now we may wonder: is it possible to personalize without a metaphorical framework? Can one experience the sky as an extension of personhood without referencing a metaphorical reality? This seems possible. Personalization is the ability to place the psyche upon the objective world, not through reference, but through manipulation of perceptual reality for the gain of existential awareness.

One gains existential awareness of the sky as something *more*, while sacrificing their perceptual reality, as they cease to see the sky as merely the sum of its parts. This is the sacrifice of personalization: perceptual disruption in exchange for existential advantage.

If one were to personalize at too deep a level, as seen in the symptoms of schizophrenia, we find that perceptual reality takes on such an existential landscape that becomes difficult to distinguish what is external from what is internal. For this reason, metaphor serves an opposite function: it provides a framework that is real and purposeful, but insofar as it aids in gaining existential awareness, much like personalization does.

Instead of allowing the vulnerability of misconstruing perceptual information that is commonplace and personalized, metaphor risks the adverse effect of getting stuck in secondary reality constructs that are only purposeful and advantageous for first-order reality. While it may seem less problematic than perceptual dysfunction, the only reason we are allowed to construct a metaphorical framework is because of its promise to gain an advantage in understanding reality. There is no substance in the metaphorical framework that is worthy on its own. When a metaphorical framework has enough substance of its own, we can consider it a reality framework. However, many times, it is assumed that a metaphorical framework is a reality framework, and thus the distinction becomes one of consciousness.

We can notice this distinction in the psyche. The psychic parts utilize a metaphorical framework that does not pertain to the wholeness of reality, but rather to a sensibility of consciousness, as if whatever the metaphorical framework is attempting to bestow is mediated through a specific psychic part that does not partake in the wholeness of personhood. For instance, poetic language has the ability to reference constructs of reality or reality itself, but its poetic prose is non-consequential to personal understanding or development. At most, poetic language offers the possibility of mending sensibilities of the heart, not understandings of the mind, because it does not reference anything on its own but rather refers to a reality framework as understood by the individual when interpreting the prose.

This is why poetic interpretation and activity, without philosophical analysis, is not worthwhile, except in its engagement of metaphorical activity and its potential to help obtain reality as it is. But it does not do enough to alter reality or shift ultimate perspectives. It can alter interactive activity and sensibilities, which in turn supercharge certain perspectives and alleviate burdens, or enable clearer seeing. The same process could have been undertaken through simple analysis of psyche parts, since all the material was already available, blocked only by sensibilities that poetry could help unlock.

This does not reduce the purpose of poetry, which is, among other things, for mending sensibilities and gaining advantage from the reality that is permeating the psyche. However, the objective of metaphor is more about gaining access to that reality than gaining sensibility of it. A metaphorical framework does not need to be emotionally infused to serve its purpose; rather, it must be referential to reality, even when fantastical, in order to be differentiated and thus elicit a particular kind of engagement.

The problem arises when an attempt at personalization is overlaid upon an already existent metaphor; an attempt to personalize an existential extension to a reality that is only serving another reality. Let's address this through an example: if we apply metaphor to personalization, such as the sky being metaphorically interpreted as heaven, and we then personalize heaven as an emotional state, we encounter a problem. Heaven is already a metaphorical, secondary order of reality, it does not retain a wholesome realness, yet we are attempting to personalize our existential reality upon that construct. The emotional state we attribute to heaven only further emphasizes the metaphorical reality against the reality it claims to inform. It enforces not our existential reality upon nature or object, but instead strengthens the metaphorical reality as a construct on its own.

This stretches the existential state of the metaphorical, second-order reality as if it were a first-order one. Religious figures often personalize metaphorical reality frameworks, and instead of gaining existential awareness, they gain metaphorical understanding in itself, against the reality it is intended to inform.

This is, again, why any attempt at personalizing political sentiment will be met with adversity, because the framework is already metaphorical. To personalize our existence upon that metaphorical construct only serves to reinforce the framework alongside its separation from the reality we are trying to form and the subjective realm we seek to develop. This is not to say we cannot personalize within a metaphorical framework, only it does not provide the personalization we're seeking. Instead, it lends greater vitality to the metaphorical framework, which only serves another first-order reality.

If that first-order reality is aligned with elements of personhood alongside aspects of reality that are proportional, then, when the metaphorical framework is personalized and given greater vitality, it will compel itself to inform those first-order reality frameworks.

For instance, poetic prose is a metaphorical reality that then informs the first-order reality. However, if poetic prose is personalized, where one attempts to place themselves within the poetic constructs, such as in theatrical performance, the informed reality of the first-order will be enlarged in proportion. For example, if someone states that "heaven" is a personalization of their exuberant states of being, then "heaven," as a metaphorical construct related to the first-order reality of their existence, will be sequentially enlarged. If heaven is metaphorically aligned to a first-order reality, such as fatherhood oversight or the unknown expanse, then personalizing heaven with emotional intensity will enlarge those first-order frameworks.

This is why religious figures who personalized metaphorical frameworks did so at the expense of the first-order realities they were meant to inform. Rather than experiencing first-order realities, like fatherhood or boundless environments, in proper proportion to the rest of life, those elements become disproportionately weighted, affecting the integrity of personhood. There are individuals who might need to experience fatherhood or vast, horizonless environments to the degree those metaphorical frameworks demand. Yet, in continually orienting themselves toward these directions, it results in an overbearing experience of first-order reality.

Even as the second-order reality of a metaphorical framework is performative in its own right, it relies on the vitality and objective of the first-order reality for its systemic viability. When the metaphorical framework changes and becomes an existential reality, it does not halt the awareness of first-order reality, rather enlarges both. Thus, one ends up dealing with a large metaphorical reality that is out of serial, so to speak, while still engaging with the elements of first-order reality that manifest without the individual's choosing.

The political framework is a metaphorical reality. Because of this, any personalization, enlargement, or attempt to render it the sole existent framework will inevitably enlarge whatever it informs in first-order reality; regardless of individual willpower. Since the political framework often metaphorically manifests in the wholesomeness of individuals, such as parental, god-like, or oversight figures, all the psychic parts that pertain to it will also be enlarged in parallel sequence.

For the sake of analogy we can imagine the case of religious frameworks as constituted metaphorical frameworks meant to access existential aspects of individuals and groups. When adhered with personalization, such frameworks become animated on their own ground. However, because the metaphor is proposing a first-order reality of existential depth, it becomes a cyclical, regenerative process. If the metaphor is adhered with too much sincerity, the first-order reality becomes enlarged to expose existential material more than the individual would like, or is capable, of handling, thus necessitating the metaphorical framework to provide an outlet away from that first-order reality. This then becomes the case of enlarging the very component one seeks to resolve.

This is why the extremity of all religiosity reaches an ironic tension, being both utopian and dystopian at the same time. The utopian version is the metaphorical framework, which then enlarges the existential behemoth that eventualizes a dystopia, only to require a more elaborate metaphysical utopia to combat its very creation. This is not to say that individuals do not retain some degree of a first-order reality, only that it is sequestered among the rest of the psyche so that it does not plague the individual.

In the overzealousness of the metaphor that is contained by the political framework, the first-order reality which to whom it targets becomes enlarged. The metaphorical process of the political realm is usually entertained for the sake of first-order realities associated with the parts of the psyche that provide oversight for compartmentalization. This can translate into constructs such as a godhead, a parental figure, the ruling class, a social class, or any other method paralleling this psychic element.

When the metaphor is utilized beyond its objective, it only serves to enlarge that first-order reality, and the psyche part meant to function as a background process of oversight becomes stricter and more assertive. This can manifest in conflicting ways: if one's oversight agenda includes responding even to minor interactive aspects, maintaining pathological harmony with all grievances of the lower systems, this is manageable at a regular pace. But when it is enlarged, as the metaphorical realm begins to exemplify its constructs, this oversight becomes unmanageable. Psyche parts and their compartments are then neglected in order to maintain this singular path of oversight.

If the interpretation of the psyche's oversight is based on parental figures, traditional frameworks, religious systems, godlike constructs, or any other horizonless potentialities of personhood, it will become further enlarged as the political metaphor pours more vitality into the first-order reality. The same process occurs, wherein, despite how the horizonless potential is interpreted or translated, it grows in magnitude, forcing the rest of the psyche to be foregrounded in service of its process.

An individual can only handle so much horizonless potential, whether this comes by neglecting certain parts in favor of others, or by facing a psyche horizon that presumes a potentiality responsible for oversight. The metaphorical vitality is the culprit behind this enlargement, which, when discussing the first-order reality, is real and must be negotiated and addressed. Not so with the metaphorical realm, which can be dismissed in a moment's notice, as it exists only to point toward something else.

As we noted with religion, we can find that when the enlargement of first-order reality becomes overdone, it begins to rely on the metaphorical realm to offset that exposure. The same is true for the political metaphor: if it has already surpassed the enlargement of its first-order reality of oversight, an oppressive oversight results, however it manifests.

To address that enlargement, a short-term solution may be to reach back into the metaphorical political framework and attempt to diminish or revolutionize the oversight aspect, which is essentially the DNA of the political framework itself. By deflecting into the metaphor, one may find respite, recognizing that by following the course of restricting the oversight character, they may lessen the burden of that first-order reality. This is true, but in gaining what they seek, they simultaneously weaken the entire metaphorical framework, merely for the sake of separating from it.

Another manifestation may occur, in which the individual reenters the metaphorical framework to seek haven from the oppressive godlike or potential force that has been enlarged. But instead of removing that force from the metaphorical structure, they entice the system to include more of that character, so that it distracts the non-oversight parts of the psyche from gaining any entrance. This distraction, enacted with such veracity, allows them to experience peace with the presumed potential, without allowing other aspects of personhood to enter that contention.

The reason that one cannot re-enter into the metaphorical framework as would the religious figure, by utilizing its utopian mindset to counter the dysphoria, is because the framework is enlarging something that has yet an opposition. While dysphoria has utopia, oversight does not have detailed orientation because the power of oversight does not allow for recognition of its opposition as detail-oriented. As well, there is no representation of the psyche system for the detailed orientation, because the details themselves cannot voice more than they are, and the attempt of oversight by enforcing weakened details would only ignore others, which will be canceled by default, even as they are more allocated for continuity pertaining to the rest of the system.

This is the danger of the political metaphor and goes for any other metaphor that reflects the oversight arena of the psyche, such as all metaphysics and theological frameworks. There is no manner to counter its enlargement other than to unveil the system of the metaphor itself. That, or simply to detach and recognize the metaphor for what it is, a non-reality framework. We are beginning to notice the cyclical pattern that has no resolve as would the utopian perspective of religious frameworks.

Chapter Four: Simulation vs. Metaphor vs. Domestication

We can gain perspective on the metaphoric realm by contrasting it with the interactive and *embodied locale*. For the context of this work, we term this locale a *domestication of public affairs*. We noticed that it is possible to construct a domestication of an entire city and/or framework; it is not limited to the usual references of domestication. The attribute of domestication we are examining is such that the entire structure is not based on substantial direction or information, but rather the interactions that underlie those substantiated tenets. It becomes embodied in a way that offsets what cannot be done outside of that domestication; that is, to become embodied in the material experience in reference to the wholeness of personhood.

We can convert this locale into an imitation or simulation of the general public which is external to it. One of the core characteristics of simulation is the degree to which one is embedded in the simulation versus the "real" reality outside of it. This becomes the most contentious and most interactive, or counter-interactive, material of that locale. Because simulation cannot be effective without the sociality that agrees to its simulating properties, it relies on and is dependent upon individuals to propagate that reality as the real reality.

A metaphor does not work in the same way; it does not rely on sociality or contractual agreement to propagate itself as a real construct, but rather gains its fertility through the informing first-order reality. Simulation does not promise to input information from outside its realm; rather, it hopes the individual will regulate their interaction with the simulation so that they can move within and deprived of the domain, thus retrieving and placing information on either side. It is upon the individual that meaning is gained through interaction with the simulation, whereas with metaphor, it is upon the metaphor itself to provide a sequence that regulates the interaction between itself and the informing first-order reality.

This means that the metaphoric realm does not concern itself with the level of interaction between the individual and its realm, for it does not rely on or depend upon sociality for its vitality. Rather, it relies on the first-order reality and the themes that naturally manifest in the individual minds. Therefore, the regulation of the metaphoric realm is not so much about the interaction of the individual contained by its realm, but rather how that realm interacts with that first-order reality. At any time, the individual can redirect or detach from the metaphoric realm, as they would from a simulating experience, but the difference is that, under the effects of simulation, it is almost impossible to completely detach because the sociality is constantly propagating its reality.

What occurs is that the individual must interact with the concurrent sociality to counter its proposition, leading to a constant tension between what they understand to be reality versus what the social environment is proposing. This does not happen in the metaphoric realm, because one is able to detach without facing opposition from sociality. Of course, there may be a sociality that ascertains a metaphoric realm, and departing from it may cause contestation from that sociality, but that is only a side effect of leaving its construct.

As with any construct, if a sociality is dependent on it, departing from it will provoke opposition. However, the natural interaction between the individual and the metaphoric realm is not antithetical, but rather an engagement between two different realms of reality. One would not feel the need to interact with the metaphoric realm in contrast to their own reality, because it is understood to be metaphorical, and they do not view the sociality as positioning itself beyond what is considered metaphorical.

Even if it is proposed that the realm is not metaphorical but rather real; take the political realm, for instance, which is positioned as a real construct of reality, if one were to detach from that position, they would not find a certain sociality that disrupts that reality. This is because, underlying their subconscious, they recognize that they are not embedded in that framework but are instead imbued with a metaphorical sentiment. This is why one can position themselves through thrilling socialities of metaphorical realms and still maintain their understanding without the sentiment that their reality is being contested.

This is not the case when dealing with simulation or interactive embodied locales. For example, the primary interactive embodied locale is the family unit. It serves as the foundational site of domestication that informs all others. Within this context, it becomes nearly impossible to separate oneself from the interactivity or reality of the environment while maintaining parallel forms of interaction of one's own choosing. While it may be possible to reduce the influence of such an environment, one cannot inhabit an embodied interactive locale and simultaneously situate themselves to be entirely distinct from it. This is because sociality exerts a continual shaping force. Even if the public sphere, potentially more authentic or truthful than a specific form of domestication, offers a different framework, the individual tends to experience their immediate embodied context as reality itself. They may position themselves in opposition to or alignment with that locale, but cannot remain neutral toward it.

This applies to all first-order reality domains, whether domesticated or not. By definition, being first-order reality means any interaction with that locale affects the individual without their ability to neutralize their own space. We may heed caution in this reality, recognizing that partaking in domestication has the mediated effect of existentially becoming part of that domain through such interactivity. The same cannot be said for the metaphorical realm, where one can engage in research or other contextual frameworks and partake in those realms without the adverse effect of becoming embedded in them or being forced to follow that framework to its end.

If one were to position themselves in the metaphorical realm without a willing sentiment of departure, the only other influence is to negotiate between the first-order reality and the metaphorical realm in which it is illustrated. One can weave and distill, in any manner they see fit, the connection between first-order reality and the metaphorical realm. However, a certain character must always be maintained, and attempts to deviate from that will only result in a conceptual overlay that does not change the effect or enlarge the boundaries of that first-order reality.

For example, the political framework will always be metaphorically aligned to enlarge the first-order reality of oversight, in whatever translational form it bears. This is because the entire character of a political realm is based on this dynamic. Changing that character would mean it is no longer a political realm, and rather something else entirely.

This is the distinction between the simulating realm and the metaphorical. The former negotiates contextual regulation of interactivity within experience, while the latter negotiates the willingness to either partake or brush it off from perspective. However, each can utilize the other's attributes to a limited extent. The simulating realm can be negotiated as a simulation and not as reality; although, as discussed, this will not be ultimately effective, yet may be enough to lessen the degree of that relation. At the same time, the metaphorical realm can be negotiated within its internal framework to develop a contextual footprint that controls how the metaphor interacts with first-order reality. Yet this too would not be ultimately effective, because the character of both the metaphorical realm and first-order reality are already molded within many frameworks and forms of sociality external to personhood. Deviation, therefore, is difficult to achieve or sustain when taken by final analysis.

It is far more difficult to construct a metaphorical realm as concrete, as one might with domestication. To fulfill the parameters of domestication, one must partake in structured organization and clear materialistic signs of its existence. To fulfill the metaphorical realm by means of a constructive value and material semblance would require symbolic formations and manipulation of material use. If one were to attempt constructing the metaphorical realm as one would a domestication, they would find themselves losing the metaphorical aspects and instead creating a domestication.

The absolute concreteness of domestication and its simulating parameters disallow metaphorical and imaginative space for expansion. This is why religious orientation is always based on symbolic construction: while it may attempt real, concrete construction, it eventually finds that it only deserves metaphorical connection and proves itself to be a domestication. In turn, religion opts for symbolic construction so that it does not deviate from its course of being metaphorically bound, yet still retains a concrete nature to prove itself as a functioning reality.

We observe that metaphorical realms which attempt to present themselves as concrete become domestications, losing their metaphorical position and instead functioning as first-order realities. Even when they postulate informational value from their metaphorical origins, they still act as first-order realities and engage with systems like any other domestication.

There may be an attempt to construct both a domesticated and metaphorical realm within the same system in hopes of alleviating each other of their limitations. However, one of two things occurs: either the metaphorical realm remains dominant, or all other concrete values personalize and reinforce the metaphorical realm, thereby enlarging the first-order reality it references, along with all the difficulties that entails. Alternatively, the domestication becomes primary, and all metaphorical values are reduced to organizational sentiment, making the realm function as a domestication with metaphorical overtones.

However, there is a problem with the latter. When one attempts to apply metaphorical attributes to a domestication, it only enlarges the domestication. What was once a nuanced experience of public reality now becomes a powerful, resilient construct that attempts to absorb every bit of public information. In such extreme domesticity, rather than offering a space of interactivity separate from the public, it becomes highly interactive, highly embodied, and disruptive to the availability of direction, regulation, or control. It becomes difficult to regulate because it constantly absorbs new information and operates with high interactivity, extracting random psyche-material to be embodied. It requires significant contextual oversight, like a mosh pit of interactivity, sending the masses into hysteria or forcing individuals into extreme perspectives just to maintain equilibrium amid all that interactivity. Additionally, this form of domestication becomes willing to participate in every public system, local or international, and becomes overindulgent in its themes.

This can easily occur where extreme domestication becomes a cult-like, which is highly interactive but somewhat lost to public interaction, and this in turn protects itself from something worse. By not having that connection, participants are simply interacting in a cyclical fashion based on one-dimensional contextual information and residual effects from the public. Thus, even though the interactivity is extreme, the direction and conscious information are not.

However, such a form of domestication that is farther from the cult is one that both has a very high level of interactivity and participates in all possible public interaction. When these two effects are bound together, it is both the case that its interactivity is not cyclical but rather newly developed; yet also erratic and dysfunctional, a form of dysfunction with high competency levels. Additionally, there is no respite from indulgence in public interaction, so every sentiment from every system which can be received results in participating in some way or fashion, leaving no availability for respite from conscious interaction.

When one examines the value attributed to objects and material surroundings under their ownership, it becomes clear that what is truly esteemed is metaphorical value, while what is merely materialistic holds structural value; meaning it is valued only for its liquidating potential or cost. It is as though one might willingly exchange all materially valuable possessions for their liquidation value to obtain other goods. There is no intrinsic value beyond this liquidatable quality; such items are merely interchangeable.

Regular domestication retains this structural character. Most of its objects, whether the home itself or its material décor, are tradable and liquidatable. Their value is based on market estimation, lacking personal recognition of deeper meaning. Ownership, in this sense, is grounded in liquidity.

This suggests there is no true ownership contained by domestication. If we treat most material surroundings as liquid assets, then even high-value property, after accounting for value attribution and subtracting the high cost of exchange, yields a relatively small, economically inconsequential return. Even the structure itself, though liquidatable at a greater sum and perceived as valuable ownership, when factoring in exchange costs, bureaucracy, and processing, results in a minimal net return. Domestication implies that all participating structures, by virtue of being part of the proper domesticated value system, will be inherently tradable due to their neighborhood and locale.

Domestication of the past cannot be the same as that of the present, because the process pertains only to the perception of externality. Since the public and external world are constantly changing, domestication, which relies on interaction with that world, cannot remain stable. This means market-attributed value to a property or structure is arbitrary, based solely on an assumed domesticated value that has already been recognized. Once the market identifies this domesticated value, it is already in the process of losing it.

The entire orientation of domestication is rooted in being siphoned off from external recognition and public consumption, processing itself instead as private and non-market-related in nature. However, once the market recognizes a domestication for its competency, it ceases to be true domestication. It either becomes a participant in externality and public discourse, thus requiring a different mode of study, or it is perceived as domestication even while no longer embodying its essential characteristics.

The market's attribution of value toward domestication is metaphorical, no different from how an individual ascribes metaphorical meaning to a material object. The market itself is metaphorical because it can only perceive value through a projected, second-order reality. It cannot access first-order reality but instead imagines a framework to justify domestication. The market's metaphor is that the property is worthy of domestication, as though it had possessed that character before its value was publicly noticed. In truth, the market cannot perceive domestication in its proper sense. Privatization does not produce sequential value from that perspective. It is almost as if we could view the market's perception of competent domestication as a metaphor for what domestication once was, but not as the reality itself, for that reality has already been surpassed.

Conversely, the market for non-domesticated entities operates within an entirely different paradigm and must be studied independently. Therefore, value attributed to domestication is not tangible, it is metaphorical. From this outlook, we can say that value pertaining to domestication reflects sentiment derived from public or private interaction rather than intrinsic worth. For the public, it is an exhibition of what domestication appears to have been; for the private, it consists of material items that signal personal development or commemorate a historicized past. Yet there is a parallel: the metaphorical value individuals place on material objects is not about the items themselves, but about connecting to a state of existence that has already passed.

This is why religious structures are cautious of excessive metaphorical value; by attaching a metaphor to a first-order reality, they risk representing themselves as something non-existent; something that only persists as a historical precedent.

For example, a competent family body will retain attributes tied to items reflecting the union of that body. These items hold metaphorical value rather than intrinsic value, commemorating what has already passed. We might say that the family body is concurrent, but more accurately, is founded upon what had originally commenced, and these material things acknowledge that. At some point, these items, or the experiences they signify, were first-order reality, not metaphor.

The early interactions between a couple, for instance, are rooted in first-order reality. However, as the family body extends itself and the union matures, interactions begin to take on the form of metaphorical value to reassert and reattribute those first-order reality experiences. This does not mean there is no possibility of gaining first-order reality, but these are dependent on childbearing and other consequential events that solidify the union in a new manner or form. These very aspects will not apply to materialistic items with metaphorical value because they are first-order reality, while bygone aspects will be available for metaphorical value.

The same is true of political structures, where some experiences of the political entity will be first-order reality, while consequential and subsequent events are metaphorical. Although the political edifice itself is largely metaphorical, which differs from other realms, there are instances when it retracts itself and enters first-order reality. However, when a political structure attains first-order reality, it is at the cost of the entire political system. To be first-order reality, it must be relatable at the individual level and available for interaction without personalization projected onto it. To do so, it must relinquish oversight and equilibrium among systems and instead platform a specific agenda and objective.

The primary first-order reality experienced at the political level is warfare and its various subsidiaries. This qualifies as first-order reality through the lived sexperience of individuals involved in warfare; though such a state does not persist indefinitely. It is not warfare itself that renders the political structure a first-order reality, but rather the system's immersion in, and reconstitution for, the possibility and structural demands of warfare that temporarily give it that character. After these periods of integration into an interactive structure centered on warfare, the political entity may lose its connection to first-order reality.

Of course, if warfare occurs within the core of the political system, where its central figures directly experience it, the condition of first-order reality may persist. However, this comes at an ongoing cost to the system as a whole. That expense increasingly binds the system to the tendencies required for warfare, ultimately permeating the entire system and preventing it from overseeing or managing other systems meaningfully.

This is why successful empires and superior state entities, over the course of prolonged campaigns, attempt to wage warfare outside their borders and beyond the sophisticated centers of political activity. If warfare were internally conducted, the system would be unable to function as a governing or overseeing body; it would become wholly integrated into the polity as a participant rather than as an arbiter.

Another way a political system enters first-order reality is through revolutionary spirit or political upheaval. In such instances, individuals adopt political agendas, sometimes for any cause, thereby transforming the system into first-order reality. When social structures adopt a political cause, the system automatically becomes a first-order reality, because participants internalize the experience as if it were their own. This is similar to the case of an autocratic figure beloved by constituents, where individuals begin to personally identify with that leader. Rather than the system remaining above or beyond individual engagement, citizens enter into a kind of union with political representatives as if those relationships were personal, thus generating a first-order reality.

Sociality creates the system in such a way that, at any moment, any form of social engagement can connect to the political sphere, thereby reducing the system through the attribution imposed upon it. Beyond mere projection and personalization toward a political abstraction, whether accurate or not, the political entity loses its oversight and attentive purpose, becoming an interactive embodiment akin to a religious system or similar institution.

It is not the seriousness of the metaphorical attribution that causes a political system to lose its character. Even if one treats a political reality as a first-order reality, that belief alone does not make it so. Rather, such a belief can offer for its metaphor vitality, expanding its references and inferences drawn from second-order reality, but this does not reduce the system to true first-order reality.

A political system becomes a first-order reality only when perception leads to political activity involving direct, relational interaction that stems from genuine first-order experience. We must distinguish these two modes because they are closely related and can transition quickly. For example, revolutionary spirit is not always the result of mistaking metaphorical structures for first-order reality; though that is increasingly common. Instead, it can arise from recognizing the system as metaphorically based, with the intent of restructuring that metaphorical foundation in order to transform the polity and its circumstances. However, often revolutionary spirit is based on misunderstanding the political system as a first-order reality and thus tied to personhood requiring change. When the system is internalized as part of personal identity yet remains an external authority, revolution emerges as the sole means of transformation.

The same can be said on the other side, where the political system, based on the choice of individuals, can be downgraded to a first-order reality without the need for revolutionary spirit. It is not that they misunderstand the system's metaphorical reality to be different than it is; rather, they make the conscious choice of ascertaining the entire political system as a first-order reality. The reason they choose to make it a first-order reality, despite understanding its metaphorical character, is because they desire a more immediate perception and experience of the personalization that accompanies its transition into first-order reality. This is the case of warfare, in which, by the choice of individuals, the edifice of the political system is downgraded to a first-order reality in order to achieve the individualistic experiences that warfare demands. It is a deliberate choice, a sacrifice of the political system and its oversight, in pursuit of an urgent objective or agenda that cannot be put off or considered to be put off any longer.

Chapter Five: The Embodiment of the Political Strata

The political strata advances according to a determined path that has all its constituents, its members, its participants become embedded in not so much the idea of something political, but more so in how it embodies itself and manifests as an acting agent in the arena where it is received as a political sentiment. This is because the embodiment is required to become truest in its form, almost beyond the representational effect of the banner that says, look here, this is the political aspect, but more so as though there is no other spectrum of experience other than this political aspect, so that it holds itself to its own standard, acting as an existential prowess of information.

This is despite the fact that it is immediately usurping the generosity afforded to normal society in its exchange and its reciprocations, where in this case it is fundamental to be outside of that and to claim itself beyond that. Because it is, after all, the emblem of a intersection of social sentiment. It is not a representation of social sentiment as though a regular banner of information, but more so in the specific aspect of being true to the intersecting nature or the conflict of consequence, where it is dealt with in this privatized spatial space.

This is because such space is without the regular sentiment that is afforded even to the representations of sociality, and it is only gaining its entrance of detail through the intersection or conflict of sociality. This is not to say that the political echelon is somehow awaiting the conflicting day, but it does not retain the tools of analysis to directly speak to social sentiment. It is not a conceptual overlay or an academic perspective, hence the idea that the philosopher and the king must depart from the same ceremony: because the king awaits the messengers of regard, and in that way the advisors or the lower echelons of the political echelon are permitting a sort of conflicting arrangement where they embody different aspects of governance so that such conflict can become presentable and then interacted in any manner that directs the information but is in no way inhabiting the information.

Although the existential parameters are significant for the political spectrum, in that there is an embodiment of persona in the political ideation, this is only because one needs to participate at a level that is beyond the conceptual arena. Since, as we noted, the political aspects are not conceptually bound, even in second-degree relationship to sociality, but instead are of their own accord, they require a certain sociality of their own to permit their existence and surely manifest their information. The truth of itself is through its orientation with itself, and in that way it finds it permissible to manifest any form of vitality. We can look at it as the extreme version of an institution that almost lives on its own without any participation with sociality, but differs very much so because it is extremely interested in sociality despite its lack of ability toward such a connection.

Such seriousness is required of the political strata to take advantage of this sort of embodiment that allows for the final realization. For example, something of political interest is foremost the representation of sociality, but in regards to the political strata it is the encapsulation of details that altogether have no pedigree, either because it is simply one piece of the addendum or because it is of arbitrary conflict; as though it can be simply the intersection of ill consequence of anything conscious-related or of social significance. The only reason that such vitality continues is that the detestable version would be the aggregation of the resentful aspects that permeate sociality, advertising the entire experience as though amidst their usual conflict, and make away with all its aspects. This would be announcing its details and concreting that experience to a point where the couple cannot flourish, for the conflict had no significance other than the haphazard stepping of toes and the immediacy of the moment. Which now the political interest has turned resentful into state-like permanence on social pariahs.

The other beneficial approach is the aggradation of that sentiment, all without the details of its connection to the underlining resentment, and very much an opt for the service of that resentment, for the political realm does not serve the emotional status of individuals or conflicts but rather its own prudence based on its internal organization. In this way the data is aggrandized, conducted, and organized according to its internal structure, embodied despite the fact that there is no sociality pertaining to it, for its connection has been severed and is followed according to that structure.

It is akin to a father observing children misbehaving and touching upon those aspects without being responsive to it, and then, in the privacy of prudent outlook, to the structure that will be overlaid upon the child. It is not fortified or vitalized from the resentful sentiment that a father may bear but more so according to that political organization, and finally through the prudence that will take effect upon the child. It may in fact be initially mentioned through the resenting sentiment, but it is very much apart from that, so that in the final prudence and enactment of fatherly discipline it is simply an aspect that follows its own structure; one that has no direct consequence or reception from the familial body, layered in a very cold and methodical manner, for there is no sociality attached to the political form at any time unless it is of a degenerate kind.

PART II: THREE PILLARS OF THE POLITIC: STRUCTURE, SEQUENCE, AND THE POLITICAL

Chapter One: Three Beliefs to Maintain a Civilized Structure

The Structural Belief: Foundations of Civilization and Consciousness

There are three beliefs necessary to maintain a civilized structure and a process of consciousness, which altogether form what we call a state society.

The primary belief, and the foundational element of any society, is the belief that there is a structural connection between that of individuals and the habitat in which they live. This we will term the structural layer, and it is the most rudimentary of all other layers. We refer to this as a belief instead of fact because we are never fully certain that there is a structural connection between one's happenstance and the environment. Instead, we rely on representational methods and physical networks, such as roads and transportation lines, which all engineer the notion that there is a structural connection.

However, it is not just a structural connection alone, but rather a social connection to that very structural reserve, so that it becomes a two-part belief: one of material structural connection and one of social connection in reference to that material aspect. The many subconscious layers that naturally interact with individuals regarding structural connections will naturally generate a sociality toward that structure. Usually, these are bundled into a single category because it is difficult for a society to differentiate between its structural connections and another sequential organization.

If there is a general sociality which does not recognize the structural connection alongside the material one, we would notice a deficiency of infrastructure, with deepening separations between physical entities, so that the physical representation does not remain intact. The primary part of a belief in a structural connection is a social sequence, which is actualized in the structural form and its materiality.

Even if we separate sociality from the structural connection, there would remain a structural representation, allowing one to fulfill a chronological belief in its vastness through the use of an imaginative layer, all in regards to the sociality that created it, even though it does not exist in real-time. Therefore, we could eliminate sociality from structural connections and still retain the belief in that sequence, since sociality is obtained via the imaginative realm and actualized in real-time through the material connection.

The opposite is not correct: if we were to remove the structural connection and only maintain a sequential form of sociality, there remains no manner of actualization. Even if there is a real-time sequential organization of sociality, it is not considered a structural connection but something else entirely. Even historical monuments which have existed for millennia can retain a structural connection based on the imaginative realm of the sociality which still pertains to it. As long as the structural connections are intact, with at least a measure of sociality (even if only in the form of an imaginative sociality), the actualization will be certain to some extent. Even if there is a relevant sociality that is sequential and evidentiary to support it, without the structural connection interworking in its outward connections, the sequential organization does not actualize and therefore is not considered a genuine structural connection.

The ability to retain through a structural connection, to ascertain the composite picture of an occupied construction, is based on the fact that actualization is the primary objective of the structural connection. Sociality and its sequential connections are a necessary consequence in order to ensure that the structural connections remain intact and are not separated or threatened by differentiated socialities. It is almost as if we do not require genuine sociality but a genuine marker to ensure that sociality will not disrupt the process and will continue to adhere to its relevance.

However, the belief in a structural connection remains as a conviction, because even as it is actualized, it is only based on one's perception at any given moment. Thus, one must believe that the structural joints continues onward, despite enough sensible evidence for that experience. When sociality differentiates and breaks down, disrupting the structural sequential output, one will engage in the connections of the structure as if they are differentiated, even as all sensibilities would point to the contrary, e.g., war, pandemic. For what makes sociality differentiate and suddenly disrupt the infrastructure itself?

Instead, we must attribute this fault to a peculiar mindset in which one believes sociality to be the container of that structural connection, as a substitute in recognizing that the structure itself is the actualization. Once one is convinced that the structural connection is more pertinent than any form of sociality, even if one turns against that structure, the sensibility toward the structure itself remains intact, undeterred by differentiated sociality. Even as sociality creates a sensibility in which there is an infrastructure differentiation due to certain actualized separations, it remains fairly futile in comparison to the general infrastructure and can be seen as solitary deviations, no different than a small construction project.

We will discuss this mindset, along with other aspects and beliefs necessary for a civilized structure. But for the structural belief itself, it shall remain intact despite notions of sociality that differentiate from its infrastructure. Unless one has evidence of sociality that is severing every transportation line, every road, every connection hub, and every point of, the structural belief will persist.

Second Belief: The Role of Political Structure in Maintaining Universal and Sequential Order

The second belief, which is encrusted upon the first and is not as principal but of significant consequence, is the belief that there is a sequential organization in nature. Without this belief, there would be a situation in which one might believe there is a localized structural connection contained by the infrastructure, but somehow does not pertain to psychic connections, universal connections, or natural connections. It would be rather a foundation of an arbitrary human form of connection, one which does not reflect back on psychic behavior nor of the intricate patterns of the universe.

Without belief in such a sequential organization, all apparent structural connections would appear subjective, rooted in the psyche, and thus confined to a fixation on infrastructure itself as the sole site for implementing and altering sequential patterns, as if it were the only domain through which to reflect on sequential form. In the usual case, where there is a belief encrusted upon that of nature and the universe, it is not so much about the structural connection itself since nature and the universe exist above and beyond. Nature's structural connections remain, irrespective of human intervention.

The structural connection in human and social construction is merely a mirror of that universality. Even if there is an appearance or necessity for terms like change, separation, or disruption, one does not have to become preoccupied with structural reconnections and recalibrations, as if that were the only matter of existence that could be molded. Instead, one notices that there is a universality of sequential organization that happens to not be married to the human structural connection; thereby, it is rather a misunderstanding, a lack of understanding, or a deficient social interaction that keeps the sequential organization perfected.

Because of the animation gained through the experience of physical connection, even if one does not have the belief in a sequential organization of nature or cosmic interference, one would still seek to ascertain as much of that structural connection as possible. When anything enters into a sequential organization, one would not will to lose that structure because of its universal fact, whether one agrees to it or not. This is similar to how the structural connection itself is a universal fact, whether one agrees to it or not. The reason we treat them as beliefs is because there is no way of knowing, at least in the sensibility of being, to these elements directly. Rather, they are complicated aspects that are both conceptually misunderstood and physically unattached.

Those who only believe in a material connection of sequential organization will follow that belief, and when there is disruption, they will seek to mend such because that is their only access to the universal reality of sequence. Those who connect to the belief in a sequential organization of nature itself, which the structural infrastructure merely mirrors to follow, will not be deterred by disruptions in the structural infrastructure, because they understand that it will retain mishaps and would not be implemented in perfect form as is the case for universal reality. This is why those who merely believe in a material connection and notice a detachment, will do everything in their power to reassert that connection; it is their only link to sequential organization. There is no limitation to their being that would prevent them from restructuring that sequence, because it is the only primacy of existence. Even when it is clearly the result of social and human mishaps or additional issues which come with infrastructure edifice, all is forgotten so that the vitality of the structural connection may be maintained.

Third Belief: The Political Sequential organization and Its Role in Stabilizing Infrastructure and Universal Order

There is a third belief encrusted upon the first two, which mitigates between them and in harmony with them: the political sequential organization. While we engage with infrastructure on one side to mirror the actualization of reality, and with nature on the other as a sequential organization of reality, there is also a third aspect: the political formation. This organization of sequence ensures that the localized infrastructure is arranged in a manner that connects itself to what is outside of that state, while also ensuring that the infrastructure is enabled and maintained throughout the internality of the state.

For if we do not have a political sequence to ensure upon the infrastructure, we may have portions of the infrastructure at any given moment which could suffer climate disruptions, separation, or breakdowns between state bodies. The political activity functions as a body to ensure that the infrastructure is maintained, protected, and that all other aspects necessary allow it to flow within the internal environment in addition to addressing external connections. This is why transportation hubs are considered some of the most politically charged entities within a state.

Because of the problematic aspect of a disruption in the sequential form of infrastructure, it falls upon individuals to place their belief system upon political entities, ensuring an agreement not only of the sociality that performs the duty of infrastructure but also in the meta-sociality between all its different parts in addition to neighboring state entities.

The belief in a political sequential form is only necessary to guide the belief in an infrastructure sequence, so that there is stability in the system and a sociality based on a sociality of all possible environments. Therefore, on a regular, moment-to-moment basis, there is no need to believe in political regulation, but rather to have it as a buffer, so that it can address complications of sociality that extend beyond individual interactions.

When an individual does not believe in a political sequential organization, what occurs is that they lack the sensibility that the infrastructure will be maintained, and there is a certain dread that accompanies the recognition of the infrastructure and its connections. For the political entity is not real in their eyes, and it is either subjugated or lacks legitimacy, or possesses all the other aspects that prevent it from being accepted. Without that belief, although there may be belief in the infrastructure and its sociality in real-time, this may not extend to the willingness to accept a harmonization of global affairs and complex sociality that extends beyond daily experience.

In this way, there is a dread to the connections that exist because of political interference. Since the infrastructure already relies on political interference, and because one does not recognize the political entity as legitimate, they become convinced that there is always the possibility of political interference with those structural connections. Almost as if the dread is created by the lack of belief, which emanates and propagates itself.

When one is forced to acknowledge the presence of a political establishment upon the infrastructure, e.g., wartime, they either agree that there is legitimacy to that entity or they recognize the political power with a possibility of interfering and disrupting that infrastructure. In this case, by delegitimizing the political entity and not recognizing its role in stabilizing the infrastructure, one will attempt to disrupt the political interference, treating it as a meddler for affairs, so that there can be infrastructure harmony. They believe the infrastructure sequence should exist as its own.

While it is true that the infrastructure is based on itself, it is only able to contrast itself and deal with the complications of sociality across state entities through the political body. In some sense, one will seek to disrupt the political interference in order to re-stabilize the sequential pattern of the natural manifestation of infrastructure, even as the political entity serves to stabilize that infrastructure. One relives the dread they fear of disrupting the infrastructure by placing an offensive upon the political entity, thinking it only diminishes the political aspect and not the infrastructure itself, when it is a disruption to both.

It is understandable that these fears arise. If the only belief maintained of the three-part system is infrastructure belief, then there is no way to backtrack to nature's sequential form, nor to backtrack from the infrastructure to any arena because that is the only animation of sequence and consciousness. Similarly, there is no way to deal with political interference, as it is not believed either, resulting in a constant dread in which the only option is to restructure the infrastructure itself by destabilizing it, thinking that the political diminishment is the cause. This is the case for the individual or group who believes in the material connection over the other two.

In the event of non-adherence to a structural sequence, one's natural sequential pattern will require another locale for admission. If their inclinations do not agree or participate in the existential reality of universal sequence, they are left with the political format as their only source of connection. And in any occasion when there is a sequential disruption to the infrastructure, they will turn to the political situation, as that is their only outlet which has thus far provided a sequential organization. This is almost the opposite of the individual or group that adheres to the infrastructure sequence and, when found disruptive, adheres deeper into that realm to ensure its sequence, even entertaining irrational suppositions. This group will deeply engage in the political framework when there is disruption to infrastructure because they have always been apprehensive about the sequence of infrastructure. Once the disruption makes itself known, they are at a loss for how to continue their vitality.

This creates a bedrock of political resentment, as they rely on the political format for the sequential pattern, and when the infrastructure fails, it appears that the political format fails as well. This causes them to be disturbed by the inconsistency of what is presented as a sequence but fails to fulfill the gap in the infrastructure disruption. In some cases, the only reason they turn to the political format is as a mechanism to provide the perfect sequential form when the infrastructure cannot, thus attributing the position of universality to it, even though the political format is only meant to serve infrastructure and its possible disruptions.

A mixture of both political resentment and political adherence causes individuals or groups to continuously move between these two objectives: first, political for providing a sequential form of experience, and then political for not providing that sequence, attributing it to some aspect that fails to make clear that the political institution is arbitrary in comparison to real infrastructure. They would like to hear as little from the political oversight as possible, but are much obliged to follow the political system and its existential practices in order to gain any semblance of a sequence.

It is this very irony that causes them to want little oversight, because of how much power they have given it, seeing it as both the father of nature and the God of the universe. Any further engagement would instantly become oppressive. One is not wary of oversight when they do not treat the subject as of any consequence to their individuality, but only in cases where it is seen as a sanctified entity; this is when they fear over-stimulation of interaction.

We will find that when these individuals or groups encounter disruptions in the infrastructure, they forget the consequential experience that led to separate from the political format. Instead, they immediately attribute the entire disruption to being politically oriented. If they were to admit that the disruption is infrastructural and separate from the political format, they would have to adhere to an infrastructure system that does not abide by or consist of the parameters of a political conception. Therefore, they immediately attribute all disruptions to political causes, despite clear evidence that political oversight typically arrives only after the fact and not as a premeditated disruption.

Even if we were to attribute all infrastructure disruptions, though this is comical in itself, to the political format, it is still the infrastructure that is disrupted and not the political objective. For example, if a political objective attempts to disrupt an entrance to a locality, but the infrastructure is stable and consistent, it will immediately find another route, without showing signs of disruption. The meaning of the disruption in infrastructure, even if directly attributed to a political objective, lies in the fact that the infrastructure itself is experiencing a fissure. We must study the infrastructure's behavior and its relevance to consciousness to understand how it constitutes itself as a disruption, but we cannot be sure that many occasions of political premeditation did not cause disruption, even if it might seem to the contrary.

One is wary of entertaining the notion of infrastructural connections because then they must assume a lifestyle and arrangement that includes systems, locales, diversity, and complexity; all of which require a significant amount of lifestyle adherence and conceptual oversight. Once one admits there is a structural system, whatever locale they find to be possessive is merely a mirror and an imagination of possession. It is part of a larger infrastructure system, of which that "dot" is merely one piece, lacking any true nuance of possession by the individual, but instead by many other attributes.

For this reason, one would not want to adhere to a structural system because it does not allow a possessive outlook or an interactive experience. This is why major religions will always be inconsistent with the agreement of a structural system. For in religion, one must be interactive with those religious points of conjecture, which create a positioned locale. If adhered to a structural system, the religious orientation would be of no consequence, and so one would rather not agree to that structural system.

Another reason for not agreeing with the structural system is because individuals adhere to the sequential organization of universality. So much so, it seems redundant, ironic, and comical to claim that a social body can create an infrastructure that is sequential and relevant in the equation of the full system. With the understanding that universality is a major, complex sequential form that transcends simple social beings, adhering to a social infrastructure as the predominant system that allows for the other two systems to come together seems as a form of downgrade.

However, because anything that is not actualized is as if it does not exist, it is only through the infrastructure itself that any relevance toward a universal sequence makes itself available. We will notice the differentiation between those who disbelieve in the infrastructural system with the proposition of a universal sequence, which far outweighs the case of a political sequence. Based on their deviation from a fissure in the infrastructure, we can be sure that if individuals or groups engage more in political rhetoric, whether resentful or positive, they owe their true sequence to the political backdrop. When they deviate to become cynical of reality and nature to adhere to a universal system of sequential organization, we can be sure that it is that realm to which they are in service, against the actualization of it.

Sequential Synergy: Structure, Politics, and the Natural Order

When an individual or group has difficulty believing in the structural sequence, they will find refuge in asserting the proposition of sequence in nature. In this case, they would rely on nature's sequential form to remain cynical about any attachment to a structural sequence, since that is always bound to social construction and its vulnerabilities. In any event where one notices the sequence in the structural habitat, instead of following the logic of that awareness, they will discount that premise based on its social vulnerabilities, which nature itself will never have to endure. The belief in the sequence of nature is used as a mechanism and refuge from structural skepticism, rather than as an adherence to that premise.

We find proof of this in the very notion that social engineering is part of the universe. If there is a sequential pattern, it should be included in the system of nature's sequences. The real reason for structural skepticism is the constant engagement with the matter itself, since it is an entire social system upon which everything else rests. There can be a philosophical justification, in which structural skepticism serves to deter the belief that structural engineering is the final product, all the while attachment of nature's sequence is not the whole picture.

They apprehension arises because they right assume that trusting a social sequence would leave them at the mercy of its direction, preventing them from retaining their theory of nature's sequence. Nevertheless, the truth is that any retention of a theory of nature will require a structural actualization. If there are fissures in the structural organization, one's adherence to the theory will be disrupted as well.

While they may assume they are retaining the sequential theory as the external realm becomes disruptive, the reality is that they are reliant on the structural sequence to continue their appraisal of nature's theory, despite their skepticism. As the structural system fails, all the theories that they rely upon become skeletal and disjointed.

If the structural sequence is fundamental, we must then consider what is secondary to it. If we claim that the sequential formulation of nature is the necessary mirror and parallel to structuralism, we risk losing the function of the political system, which provides a genuine structural input. Even as we have mentioned that the political system hovers above the structural realm to facilitate its development, certain elements of the political body are compulsory inputs for the structure itself. The political body has the ability to unify, which the structural system does not. Without sensible unity within the structural system, it will fail upon its differentiation.

In the ideal scenario, unity arises when individuals and groups adhere to the structural sequence for its own sake and for the theory of nature itself. In doing so, simply adhering to the sequence, they experience unity, especially since they are nearly of similar composition. However, this expectation is often unmet because the very manifestation of the structural system is its universality and diversity, which cannot be reduced to any simplistic political premise, and in some sense, it is nationless. This is where a political input provides a semblance of unity. Although limited to the nation-state and disruptive to the international notion of structuralism, it offers an arbitrary brushstroke to remind of the constituency of unity that is not reliant upon the structure itself.

In cases where identity is in question, the political function will enter consciousness and serve as the unifying measure until it fades into the background, allowing real structuralism to manifest.

Thus, the political function does include itself in the structural system. Though, it is only an addition, not an ingredient in the structural manifestation, so it remains a body that is not a core part of the system. To understand which of the two, universality or political, is secondary, we need to explore the inclusion of the universal sentiment within the structure itself. This inclusion is more subconscious, as the structure requires a theory of nature to mirror its function, remaining constant as the blueprint of the system but never becoming more than that.

If the theory becomes conscious, it will always come at the expense of the structural system. This is because a conscious theory of a sequence of nature will make the mere social construction appear insufficient and, moreover, not the genuine system. Also, to appear in the conscious realm would require that the imposition of having the sequence of nature becoming personified, so that it is included in social dynamics. Whenever we personify a theory of nature within the structural system, we only create an affair in which that personification is one among many social dynamics.

As an individual, it must adhere to the limitations of individuals, so the entire premise of the theory, as a sequential pattern of nature, becomes realized in a structural setting as a personification, in which it is merely a part of the sequence. Because of that adherence, the theory realizes itself as a sequential pattern that is antithetical to its embedded structure and thus both non-sequential, treated as a mere avatar of social dynamics, and, secondly, it appears resentful toward the structural system, limiting itself to a non-sequential actualization, as if the structure does not want to perceive it as sequential. This is why the theory of nature must remain in the background to facilitate the construction of the structural system. Once it becomes a conscious player, it leads to the theory's demise.

However, the opposite can also occur, where the structural premise does not follow a pattern of nature for its sequential organization. In such cases, the structure loses the parameters that define a sequence. While the political input would not harm the system as much, the introduction of nature's sequential form would only personify and add no substance to the system's engineering. Thus, the structure relies on a subconscious input with that theory in mind to maintain the system. Because it cannot become conscious, the development of that theory and its input must be an enterprise conducted outside the system.

In this way, the religious construction that postulates and develops this theory is paramount as an assigned substance from the external realm, so that it sometimes reinsulates that premise into the conscious system. Usually, the external religious faction is wary of the consciousness system for being a structural sequence opposed to that of nature and universality, so convergence between the two is difficult. However, if we observe the development and stimulation of external religious factions, they are engineered by the consciousness system itself, given availability to develop only because that is the required constituent for the system. When there is enough input into the consciousness system, it will cease to allow or stimulate development of that religious premise for fear it will input at a level that makes itself consciously known to the system. In this way, if there is a rise in external religious simulation, it suggests that the conscious spectrum requires input to its subconscious layer; when there is a decline in religious simulation, it indicates there is enough input of the theory for the structure to continue properly.

We need to avoid personifying the consciousness system as if it were a call to action rather than a systemic aspect. The system is merely a process that mirrors nature's universality and its parameters, signaling necessities based on its evolution. It is not "alive" in the sense of being personified; it only follows the rules on which it is grounded. Once one understands these rules, they can navigate the system as they see fit. If we notice a personification of consciousness, it is only because a certain parameter is being met so intensely that it appears as if the system were being personified. The system's rules can seem personified when its necessities are unmet, with the capacity to bring disaster, not because it holds resentment or any other intent, but simply because its parameters have been activated in a way that causes it to appear resentful. We may think the system concerns itself with individuals, but that is not true; it does not form attachments but only propagates itself according to the social engineering that mirrors nature.

The universality of nature, which, as we have noticed, is a mere theory placed upon the structure, becomes actualized in the system and begins to act personified. The structural system is not personified, and this is the foundational layer of the whole enterprise, only the actualization of that universality of nature begins its actualization. This actualization allows that sequential pattern to gain a certain political stance. Just as the political body is a system that follows the structural one, placing an identity upon it for provision and protection, the actualization of nature upon the structural system is of the same kind. It gains the advantage of a universality of nature that begins to regulate the structural system, for the same effect of providing provisions and protections.

The reason political and universal spheres are not redundant is because they offset each other. When the political body provides provision and protection with too much earnestness, the universal actualization disrupts the political power; and when it fails to provide provision or protection, the universal actualization begins to provide such. The reverse is also true: the political body offsets an overbearing universal actualization by disrupting the input of that theory. Also, in cases where there is a lack of input of the theory into the system, the political body will either provide its constitutional power to input notions of that theory or assist in grounding the input of the external religious systems into the conscious system.

We cannot always identify which layer is the premise of a conscious personification, for disaster can arise from any of these premises. The structural system itself may engineer a particular pathway, with the parameters themselves being the reason for that occasion. There is no personification, for it does not reflect but rather follows its rules. It may be the case that the parameters of a structural system have been met, and because the other layers decide against that premise, they disrupt the system itself.

For instance, an epidemic can emerge from the parameters of the structural system; however, the political body may disrupt that perpetuation because it seeks to provision and protect the structural system. Yet it may also be the case that the political body seeks to provision and protect against the needs of the structural system, so that, instead of offering protection for the system, it acts on behalf of the individuals contained by it, against the system itself.

Epidemics are particularly pertinent to this discussion because the political body has the ability to disrupt the entire structural system on which the epidemic depends, thereby neutralizing its capacity to cause harm. In such a case, the political body is no longer acting as protector and provider of the structural system, but rather against it. The outcome is a corrupt political body and a major disruption of the structural system; both at a loss.

However, there is a third layer in this situation: following the emergence of an epidemic, understood as a manifestation of structural parameters, universal actualization can either assist in the spread or protect against its effects. If it chooses assistance, appearing to agree with the premise of that structural parameter, it may spread the epidemic further, engineering more change than that of the non-personified structural system would.

If that occurs, the political body will almost certainly act against both the structural system and the theory of universality. Rather than functioning in its intended capacity, it becomes oppositional to both. This would cause the entire enterprise to collapse: the structural system would lose its premise, the theory on which it depends would be undermined, and what would remain as the sole mainstay of society is the political system.

Another example is war, which often manifests as a deterrent to the political body. When the political body is deterred, it cannot provide for or provision the structural system, and may even actively disrupt it. In such cases, the structural system will experience deep dissonance with the political body at war. Even though the political body's premise is to protect and provision for the structural system, once the system is affected, that premise has failed.

Consequently, the structural system may begin to reject the political body as a deterrent to its development even if the political body once served its objectives. This may foster a desire to create or dismantle political power, depending on how it interacts with the structural environment. Conversely, the structural system may respond to the failure of the political body by acting in a political manner to ensure political continuity. But in doing so, it loses its own premise, calling into question the political body's very necessity; what good is a political system without a structural foundation to provide for?

Thus, the usual outcome of war that affects the structural habitat is that neither system fails because of war itself, but rather due to the structural system abandoning its position and merging with the political body.

When the entire enterprise is disrupted, what remains of the three layers will form the basis for renewal. Any of the three may enable a comeback, depending on the nature of the decline. For example, if the collapse stems from the theory of universality disrupting the structural system, then what remains is the political body. If the collapse is within the political body, what remains are the structural system and its theories. No one layer alone, neither theory, structuralism, nor political sequence, is sufficient to construct a civilized structure. Full formation requires all three. Structural sequence is the most difficult to establish because it requires a genuine investment in complex sociality, one capable of competently mirroring universality.

The difficulty of a major structural disruption lies in its renewal, particularly when reliant on the political body. This would also require a form of sociality capable of stabilizing the parameters of the structural system, allowing it to flow in reflective cogitation. However, a newly renewed complex structure may become its own demise, carrying with it the complexity of a sociality unfamiliar with its lineage. The structure may be used against its own premise, applied through efforts misaligned with its original intent. This leads to fragmented process and a disruptive outcome, as the structural system attempts to function alongside a sociality that neither understands nor adheres to it.

The truth is, a renewed structure must align with current sociality, so as not to introduce more complexity than can be absorbed. Structural change, however, is slow. It falls to sociality to offer a renewed consciousness, one that the structure can mirror. If that consciousness does not emerge, the structure's parameters will act to prevent misuse. Because sequential sociality arises not from the structure, but from the political body and universal theory, the structural system will begin to resist both. This resistance can be seen as a kind of revenge; a response to the political body that initially caused structural harm.

Such resistance may take the form of political disruption, leading individuals to abandon adherence to the political sequence and retreat into the structural layer. Yet this response depends on the individual. If one takes the failures of the political system too seriously, they may attempt to reform it, ignoring the needs of the structural system. In disrupting the political system, the structural habitat risks bringing about its own demise, as individuals become absorbed in political concerns.

This is where the third offset, the sequential pattern of nature as mirrored in the structural system, becomes important. It can foresee such developments and reassign power to the political body, mediating disruptions from the structural layer to prevent individuals from abandoning it entirely.

The political body, in turn, can work to block the theory of universality from gaining conscious orientation within the structural system. It may do so by regulating population flow or its diversity. Through these measures, the personification of universality becomes less viable, as diversity exposes competing perspectives within the system.

By virtue of diversity, a dynamic space emerges that resists a singular sequential personification. Though one might attempt to dictate such a personification, the presence of diverse, sequential individuals makes it appear absurd. When individuals do not align into a cohesive sequence, any theoretical sequence of universality, especially one lacking materiality, faces the same consequence.

This is why highly religious societies may resist dynamic exchange, not simply due to existential unease (as noted in other works), but because the theory of universality is personified. Any interaction that introduces differentiation destabilizes the theory itself.

Thus, even simple political regulation of population flow can offer the political body leverage: by creating diversity that disrupts the personification and conscious realization of the theory of universality. Of course, the political body may also maintain population control to preserve sociality, which benefits infrastructure.

When the theory of universality gains too much conscious control over infrastructure, it produces a sense of futility or vanity within the structural system. Critiques of certain societies often stem from the overdevelopment of that theory, which proclaims itself superior to the system, casting the infrastructure as primitive or insufficient. The contrast becomes natural: universality begins to question and destabilize sequential aspects of infrastructure, deeming them worthy of disassembly.

This occurs because the disparity between the two layers becomes too stark. The choice between them becomes clear, one toward a decaying infrastructure, the other toward a perfected sequential form. Universality, in this state, becomes domineering, forgetting that it is merely a theory, enabled only by the infrastructure itself. As noted, the political body may intervene, via population control or by detaching individuals from the idealized form, in order to protect the infrastructure itself. This is not ideal for the infrastructure, as it would mean that instead of the proper proliferation of sequence, the political body would sweep in and disassemble specific social bodies embodying the theory of universality, which has gained enough traction to disrupt the infrastructure. However, this is necessary, as the alternative would be to allow the disparity to gain greater traction, leading to the eventual embodiment with the consequence of disrupting the entire infrastructure, which would be perceived as being of such low quality compared to the idealized version encountered.

We must remain vigilant to remember that it is not the expansion of the theory of universality, this work is a far stretch in that category, but only the belief that it is a genuine version of reality, instead of a theory that originates from the infrastructure and is always inferior to it. For example, we are noting three layers of a complete civilized system, but this is only based on a theory of sequential organization of universality, not a manifestation of the structural system. Just by virtue of our reflection, we can be dispelled from the camp of the structural system, so that we are only made possible by the structural layer and all that it entails. For this reason, it can be the case that this work may be problematic for infrastructure, as it does not stem from its necessities and can be used against it. It would then be upon the political body to disrupt the dissemination of this work so that the infrastructure can maintain its prowess without the theory of universality gaining conscious awareness.

This brings us to a crossroad: how can we make conscious what is required to remain subconscious within the infrastructure? This is why the proper utilization of what is external to the infrastructure is crucial for an improving interaction with it. As with sexuality, we may follow its dynamics intuitively, but conscious awareness of its theory can also help us optimize its function. How could we develop intrinsic infrastructure if we had only its movements, but no reflective context?

Thus, the theory of universality must offer that context, allowing development within the infrastructure. However, this information should not enter the infrastructure consciously, just as someone engaging in sexual dynamics does not include all their research in the act of such. Rather, it should develop the subconscious via the conscious, only to return to the subconscious when interacting with the system.

Thus, we can say that a generation of philosophy also requires the betterment of the theory so that the infrastructure may have a chance for change. However, we have noted that throughout the ages this very philosophy can be used to disrupt the infrastructure, and we need not look far for examples. The point is that the input and interaction through infrastructure must be devoid of this research, focusing instead on the continuity of its system with humility.

PART III: INSTITUTIONAL STRUCTURES

Chapter One: Institutions, Consciousness, and the Architecture of Exchange

Institutional structures require a definition that is more nuanced than what initially appears. Just as a culture or identity devises institutions, a physical locale partaking in and provoking social and market exchanges of materials that serve as the foundation of their thesis, so too are existent institutional formulas. For an aspect to be animated in the social environment, there must be a perpetual exchange of social sentiments and market items. This exchange may seem arbitrary, since the material is already within the system, and one might assume that the same item changes hands in a cyclical fashion. However, we might forget that most market exchanges use the same currency that changes hands in a cyclical manner. The individual retains a degree of currency only to exchange for something else, until another exchange occurs and the same currency is regained, and this process never stops. The underlying mechanism is the exchange itself, rather than the material being offered in exchange. The real value in exchange lies in the real-time presence of that exchange, which activates social interest by means of interaction to create dynamism in the material in addition to conscious sentiment.

Exchange is based on the recognition of a restraint for distinct variables to succeed in every department of biological necessity or conceptual expansion.[ii] The exchange is negotiated based on the materiality of an item and how it contrasts with the proponent's offering, all while it is the social context that provides the framework. The contrasting material to the exchange value is a term that is set by the social environment. When an item is scarce, especially a biological necessity, it provides a greater contrast, and the exchange value is determined accordingly. Even conceptual amenities are influenced by social context, and may be the sole determinant, e.g., comfort.

Therefore, even when a concrete exchange is provided by the limitation of an individual's expertise, as in *politics,* it is the value of contrast that provides the context for exchange. A value can be a determinant of zero and be removed from the table of exchange, while other seemingly devalued items can be introduced, depending on the social context. This allows us to sum up the entire element of exchange, whether market or conceptual, into the realm of sociality, determined by contrasting material, and thus the value and ability of exchange.

The determining factors of sociality, in terms of contrast, are primarily the conscious sentiment of that sociality, or the conceptual contemplation at the present moment. We agree to the premise based on conceptual convenience, as change occurs rapidly in alignment with the conceptual agreement of the present moment. Because it is conceptual, and owed to the sociality which expands the contemplation of conceptual data, it will always be the case that the primary factor for contrasting an exchange value is the exacting consciousness of that sociality.

We can imagine an individual who is wrapped in a conceptual amenity that is not agreed upon by the social context, for which it may either be exchanged for a zero-sum value or a value that cannot be determined. By default, zero-sum relegates the exchange to be inconsequential for the rumination of current consciousness. This does not mean it is impossible as a medium for a certain individual, but in terms of the necessary consciousness of the moment, it is not an essential aspect. There is the possibility of a buffer between the current consciousness and the market exchange, but since the social context is still undetermined regarding the exchange value, the consequential process for individual consciousness does not materialize. Whatever appears to be received at zero-sum will inevitably fade with time because of its inaccessibility to current consciousness.

The second point of biological necessity, such as food scarcity, would appear to suggest that the determinant value is in reference to the organism's necessity for survival. However, we may not follow closely enough to notice that in a scenario of complete survival, the notion of market exchange would cease to exist. As long as there is an exchange, there is a populace adhering to a certain contextual sociality that assigns value to that exchange. When the organism values food in a scenario of food scarcity, part of their psyche adheres to the contextual value ascribed to it. Surely, there is a portion that values the necessity of food sustenance, but when removed from the social value, the availability of sustenance increases significantly.

We can imagine three major junctures in this scenario: First, there is food availability, where the value is clearly marked by conceptual agreement, with the possibility of zero-sum with certain food items. Then, there is the stage of food scarcity, where the conceptual agreement diminishes but retains a certain contrasting hold on value, even if zero-sum food items seem absent. Finally, there is the stage where whatever sustenance is available must be confronted, with no political or other social system for a conceptual overlay.

This can be misleading, for the individual's state can be so desperate that biological necessity becomes the only mechanism urged towards sustenance. However, by being under a political or similar system, their conceptual overlay will determine their food choices based on contrasting value, even if it leads to their detriment in doing so. The mere conceptual overlay affects the exchange value, compelling the individual to partake in that exchange even when seemingly zero-sum food items are within reach. A profound individual might take notice of this and detach from the system to follow pure biological necessity, partaking in the zero-sum food items. There is always the possibility of relieving the conceptual system, where an entire margin of the system becomes available at a zero-sum value, with no competitors in sight. We may be unaware of how determinant the conceptual system is upon the perception of value and exchange.

What is most attached to personhood becomes most unavailable for exchange. When compelled for exchange, such as in warfare, it is the result of a conceptual framework: like a political institution, which takes charge of the exchange, with the ability to exchange a life for political defense or offense. Had the individual of political exchange detached from their adherence to the conceptual system, they would immediately become unavailable for that exchange. This is the institution of war: to enable combatants to partake wholeheartedly in the political institution, making themselves available to its value attribution at the expense of their own lives. Self-sacrifice is only possible within a conceptual framework, for the biological framework is solely concerned with propagation and survival. In this context, courage is the ability to attach to the conceptual framework despite biological demands.

Even the material of the exchange is arbitrary to the real-time benefit; only the conscious sentiment is the absolute value of it. The conscious sentiment is an appropriation of the political, social, and identity systems which espouse a certain constitution. Both the constitution and the consciousness it creates work in tandem to form psyche rumination. Without the constitution of an identity, it would cease to function as a working conceptual framework. Without a conscious sentiment, it would not operate as an embodied version of the constitution. The conceptual framework is not dynamic until the particulars of society exchange that material to produce a conscious sentiment.

The difficulty of creating a dynamic exchange of participants lies in the deviating nature that plagues the psyche. To be interested in dialogue which correlates to the constitution will manifest as a subsequent decline to that very constitution; with no guarantee of the constitution's longevity and its conscious sentiment. However, when we factor in a marketplace of exchange, we create what we are defining as an institution, which serves that function. Although the exchange of ideas related to the constitution, for instance, political discussion, may not produce an adequate exchange due to its lack of association with the entire societal body, it can still contribute to the real-time effect of dynamic exchange, allowing a form of self-consciousness pertaining to constitution to eventually enter into the market of real exchange.

When we study the actual market, we notice that what is chosen to be exchanged is not necessarily the needs of the constituents, but rather what provides excellence for the real-time manifestation that makes dominant constitutions a reality. One may invent services or products to be included in the market exchange, even if they have not been requested or are of no real utility other than their potency for exchanging a conscious sentiment aligning with important constitutions.

When those constitutions decline, the corresponding sentiment, and finally the product or service, will be annulled from real market exchanges. Everything in the market participates in this process, and even what is assumed to be raw necessities is thoroughly embedded in a prominent constitution. Even the concept of housing for higher life forms is part of the primary constitution that maintains conscious sentiment.

When adherence to these constitutions, which are embedded in the political body, weakens, even the notion of housing will be less considered as a normal fact of life. When we conceptually and physically depart from civilization, (both departures being necessary) we begin to follow a stream of declining consciousness that loses the matter-of-fact of housing. Abstract thought of any kind will not be available in such a departure, as even deliberate thought is thoroughly intertwined with constitutions and conscious sentiments that cogitate within institutional structures.

Although it would take a complete disconnect for a true "feral-man" state to take effect, we would still witness its declining potency with a limited attachment to housing. I have noticed that in such a desert realm, I lost the ability to naturally attach to the sentiment of housing as a normal function of life. Because housing has been embedded in the structure of civilization for a prolonged period, it becomes easy to invoke a conscious sentiment within the populace.

Yet, we find a correlation between competent and incompetent housing that allows us to identify individuals who lack the advantages provided by civilized constitutions; those frameworks that espouse certain sentiments and enable particular ways of life. Far from the core of civilization, housing becomes nearly ironic: an assumed necessity whose futility is tacitly understood, yet still maintained because it remains, fundamentally, an amenity to be experienced. And yet, that amenity cannot be fully accessed by those who do not understand housing as a conceptual sentiment; who cannot participate in its deeper implications.

Comfort, in this context, is indicative of a residual consciousness, one that is lost or inaccessible to those detached from the sentiment of housing. For such individuals, housing would not be comfortable, because the conscious sentiment required to engage meaningfully has been eroded. It becomes perplexing, then, when individuals attempt to access the amenities of the wealthy, presuming they can achieve that level of conscious sentiment through market exchange, while lacking familiarity with the notion that gives those amenities meaning.

Enter the institution: a public domain wherein members participate in conscious rumination, serving simultaneously as a center for market exchange. The educational institution, for instance, engages in the exchange of educational material that reflects the conscious sentiment of the political constitution. Within such institutions, we may find sub-constitutions, distinct but related sets of parameters that govern their internal functions. However, these sub-constitutions are always tethered to the broader political constitution, either in alignment or in contrast.

For example, the educational institution may carry a sub-constitution dedicated to the cultivation of children's potential. This sub-constitution cannot be separated from the political constitution; rather, it is either a manifestation of its values or a counterpoint. Most educational institutions emphasize disciplined conceptual frameworks, reflecting the broader conceptual order of the polity. One could argue, then, that the educational institution's purpose is to give credibility to such frameworks, which in turn upholds the political constitution as a conceptual form.

Before the advent of educational institutions, political entities were not experienced through conceptual frameworks. Monarchy, or other forms of governance, existed as systems rooted in biological necessity, formed and followed instinctively. The king, for example, was not seen as a component of a system of governance, but rather as a central figure in a way of life.

The philosophical introspection that allowed us to understand the political system was a method to incorporate the concept of conceptual frameworks into political reality. This, in turn, necessitated educational institutions to continuously engage in the market exchange of real-time conceptual frameworks. In this sense, philosophy generated the conceptual framework that birthed the political one. And in turn, the political system required institutions, schools of philosophy and education, to stimulate the ongoing vitality of the polity. Wherein original philosophy aimed to create and expand conceptual frameworks, subsequent philosophy became increasingly preoccupied with their internal exchange, especially in service of political continuity. The focus shifted from qualitative exploration to real-time exchange alongside diverse constituents.

The initial, qualitative aspects of educational material, those that go beyond providing frameworks and aim toward the progressive enlargement of consciousness, serve a different purpose than institutional goals. That form of quality is aimed at distributing consciousness throughout the psyche. However, that is not the topic at hand, so we will not pursue it further.

The exchange of ideas within the institutional framework differs starkly from individual or group exchanges, primarily because of the lack of a constitution in the social dynamic. Although friendship groups can be elaborate in exchanging vital information, because they do so from a personal basis, they do not instill a constitution a purposeful exchange. Only when the group has been institutionalized to serve the exchange of the constitution will it provide dynamism to it. For instance, if a family or individual hosts a gathering or communion in their home, they do so from a certain constitution. Typically, this is under the rubric of an identity that espouses the conceptual basis of hosting, through which the dynamic exchange provides dynamism to the constitution of that identity and its sub-constitutions of hosting.

Another constitutional aspect of hosting may involve appropriating various elements of the family body for engagement with society, or for fulfilling psychic needs not met within the family. In this way, the exchange aims to enhance the family structure or its position in society, but it does not offer vitality to a broader institutional framework.

We might say that one utilizes the institution of the family body, but we would be misusing the term "institution." The family body is not an institution in the sense that it elaborates the personal realm. The constitution of the family body is ever-changing according to the individuals that make up that personal domain. Just as the personal realm does not remain fixed or categorized, sequencing its psychological movements, so too is the family body not bound to a single constitution but continuously changes in real time.

When we refer to the institution of marriage, conversely, we are speaking of a more formal constitution, one that sets parameters for how the family body will be domesticated according to socially constructed rules. This is not the constitution of the deliberations within that domestication, but rather a constitution for the form of domestication itself, one that facilitates private exchanges of private material. Thus, we must speak accurately: the institution of marriage is best understood as an institution of domestication. Even those who forgo marriage maintain a constitution of domestication if they engage in any form of intimate or domestic exchange. The terminology may differ, the legal or cultural bindings may vary, but the underlying structure remains.

The institution, as we have discussed, can be understood as a site of market exchange for the real-time activation of a constitution, or as a means of engaging with what is otherwise non-interactable. A constitution is a complex system of ideas that follows a specific format for both individual personhood and the collective. Because it exists as a conceptual structure, it cannot be directly interacted with; it requires a physical realm to act as a gateway to the conceptual database. These gateways function as "humanized" versions of the idea, even when that translation appears obscured or incomplete.

A constitution is not easily accessible as a directive for complex systems. For instance, an individual might embrace a personal constitution to avoid causing harm to others, but this cannot be consistently applied due to the intricacies of social dynamics and self-preservation. Large volumes of philosophical thought are required to unpack such complexities and their connection to constitutional principles. After philosophical introspection, one must dissect the credibility of the constitution to understand its underlying sentiment. To apply the constitution accurately, it must be understood at a level that allows interaction with all aspects that must be considered for making proper choices. Due to the near impossibility of accurately applying any constitution, it is necessary to have a separate realm that attempts to institutionalize its details or market exchange, so that its credibility can be delivered in manageable quantities, allowing the individual to understand the constitution in its applicable nature.

The justice system, for example, is an institution that provides a perspective on the constitution by analyzing the most extreme cases of social exchange that test the limits of following or not following the constitution. More fundamentally than the service of justice, the institution serves as a domain that indulges in competent social exchange, physical and conceptual, in its sole purpose of outlining aspects of the constitution.

Theoretically, a political system need not maintain a centralized justice system. Local disruptions could be handled without institutional involvement. Indeed, in the peripheral zones of many states, this is often the case, where neglected regions self-regulate outside the purview of the official justice system. This illustrates that the justice system primarily functions as a locale for constitutional deliberation, rather than a universal provider of justice. In such systems, constituents often become law material, rather than recipients of justice per se.

What serves as most Just is the applicable nature of the constitution, which does not presume the constitution to be Just in it of itself. Under the assumption that the constitution is the proper approach to life, such as freedom, justice will determine when and how it should be applied on a social level. To be unjust would be to derail that constitution, to assume an aspect of it without considering all the moving parts. Choosing not to follow the constitution from the outset would not be unjust, but rather an act of treason or ignorance of the political establishment.

Chapter Two: Political Institutions and Constitutions

The government is established to fulfill the need for a political or universal institution. Contrary to its premise, the government does not govern the populace; it merely enables a stalwart position that significantly affects its citizens. The more citizen-like the individual, the more interested the government is in them. The government provides a platform for the primary citizens and, in doing so, grants them the opportunity to interact with the constitution's conscious sentiment. It does not concern itself with the managerial aspect of governance, as that is naturally appropriated by the social structure itself.

When the government appears to be governing, it is only stabilizing its institutional position above all else. Once that premise is secured, the government recedes into the background as a mere institution for citizen interaction, devoid of conscious engagement with individuals or groups. The appearance of governance stems largely from the primary citizens being connected to the institution, which succeeds the social structure in following the conscious sentiment of that constitution. Most state management is driven by social demand and expectation. Those outside of powerful social influence may pose a threat to the state's management, but not to its governance.

The government does not concern itself with individuals unengaged with the social structure, as they lack the conscious sentiment necessary for interaction. They do not possess the social connection required to engage with the government institution, let alone influence the constitution itself. Any perspective they hold on the state is a conjured supposition with no basis in real-time movement.

The institution continues the material of the constitution through general social exchange. The items exchanged represent the constitution, and the intellectual property contained by these exchanges is the material embedded in the identity of the government. However, the content of the exchange holds no significance for the constitution itself. Even if the same item moves back and forth between social agents, it does not constitute an institutional requirement. The same holds true for sophistication and complexity; complexity in exchange does not enhance the preliminary constitution.

Surrounded by a religious identity, we find institutions of both the first and second kind, though their differences do not produce a more dynamic form of life. A university, for example, enhances complex ideas and offers an abundance to the social environment, but not to the base of institutional needs. A university is a constitution of education, and its defining institutional factor is the vitality of education as a whole, despite its materialized elements. A university may have superior material resources yet be worse off as an institution of education. Conversely, another university might provide a more dynamic educational exchange and therefore be considered a fairer institution of education. The process of exchange in universities involves a multiplicity of ongoing educational dialogue. A university in which all members continuously exchange educational sentiments in a dialogical format would be considered the epitome of an educational institution.

However, every institution must also engage in an exchange with the broader institutions of society. An institution grounded in, say, religious identity may be complete on its own, yet if it does not participate in the marketplace of broader societal and political institutions, it cannot be considered animated in a universal sense.

The institution of education retains the dynamism of education, yet education itself is not a constitution that can directly enter the domain of sociality. Educational sentiment is contextual information that may or may not assist in sociality depending on the moment's demand. The constitution of education lacks social exchange and consequentially must be withdrawn from society for remote attention. This also necessitates that it be occasionally paused in order to experience sociality without the burden of that contextual overload. Accessibility becomes as important to education as content, since the constitution does not organically integrate into sociality.

Choosing to depreciate the constitution at proper intervals allows for the possibility of normal sociality against that constitution. Sociality, in this context, refers to the interactions most centered in the psyche; for instance, the familial body. The difficulty of having sociality as a portal into the medium of society with normal market exchange either demands irrelevance to all contextual information or, worse, provides a haven for emphasis on a single item from the contextual material to prove oneself worthwhile in the market exchange. The chosen item is usually a quick assessment of the demand of market or social exchange, and not due to any former attachment to it.

Although one may contain a reservoir of material, at the first instance of a market or social demand, one chooses a very specific part of the material to ascertain their position in that thoroughfare. However, this can be unscrupulous because the educated material is not a database for social or market usage. Rather, it is an overview of systems that cannot be reintegrated into systems; like how an art provider, such as a poet, cannot place poetic sentiment into the practical aspects of the material. We may wonder about the relevance of partaking in the material when sociality does not provide a method of exchange for it. This is the reality of the material, as unexchangeable for normal social dynamics. The material is only helpful in enlarging the interactive experiences, to provide, as we have termed it thus far, context for substance, not to be considered substance itself, but to offer insight that will garnish the already present substance.

We have accorded an understanding of a constitution that cannot be placed into sociality. We may wonder whether all constitutions share this characteristic, being imitations of a social aspect but not accessible to sociality. The primary constitution is the political one, which exists in various forms. However, it will always be a constitution of a geographic populace. This means it follows an exemplified version of the organization of people but does not "represent" the people. The constitution is a created thesis of a system of people but does not stand for the representation of individuals or the ruling class contained by social dynamics. The constitution is always differentiated from the populace because it is only an exemplified version of them in political forums.

Therefore, the constitution should not be reinserted into sociality, because it is only exemplified and not a true basis for any social dynamics or even market exchange. The market will demand according to the needs or reciprocation of the populace, irrespective of the political constitution. Social-philosophical exchange will be in accordance with sociality, which, though affected by the constitution, is in no way a manifestation of it. The constitution may serve as a cause for the philosophical needs of the people, for instance, in a democracy, the individual will usually require a sense of participation in all areas of life.

However, the individual may also require other conceptual aspects that do not pertain to or cannot be explained through that constitution. Even the previous example is more a rebalancing of the cost of democracy than a direct causation of the constitution itself, since every constitution limits certain aspects that require attention in normal sociality. For instance, the constitution of education causes it to be remote from social conversation, and as such, will always be the case that the educated class will involve a more interactive sociality. We would not say that the educational constitution is the determining factor in that class participating in a more in-depth sociality, but rather that it is a response to having been forsaken.

We see another case in the political constitution, which does not enjoy the advantages of social exchange. Therefore, even after participation in the political constitution, one cannot coalesce such material into the realm of social dynamics. For instance, in a democracy, a constitution of majority or individual power, would not be appropriate to carry those forms into personal social dynamics. If this were to manifest in totality, then a familial body might be ruled by the majority, namely, the children, against the conscious aptitude of the parents. The same could be said of education, which, if modeled on the majority rule, would favor the students rather than the educators.

We cannot assert that children and students have chosen a specific political forum, but rather that they are bound to the necessities of normal social exchange, which requires a different structure than that of democracy. Another instance of a political constitution that cannot be replicated in social dynamics is the concept of rights emanating from the state. Social exchange could not be about the rights of each individual exchanging material or its market-related elements. Rights from the state are designed to administer a certain oversight of social exchange, but we would not say that friendships are based on the rights of each party. Not even moving into philosophical argumentation about social exchange being based on rights, it is enough to say that if the political constitution were replicated in social exchange, it would undermine normal sociality. Sociality is not defined by such a constitution; instead, it is defined by the exchange itself based on the demands and needs of the participating members, irrespective of constitutions. Each individual may claim a right toward another, but that immediately uproots the dynamic from being social to entering into a political structure.

This might be appropriate during the social exchange of political figures, but quite alarming in the exchange between family members. If this replication of constitutions continues undeterred, political exchange will seem familial, and familial exchange will seem political. The constitution, assumed to be applicable to daily life, would cause the most complex social dynamics, those among family members, to take the route of a narrowed political constitution. Meanwhile, the constitution of marriage, or familial domestication, may be replicated in the political sphere, assuming that such depth of personhood should be applied to the entire political institution.

Let us consider another example to illustrate this point: the institution of marriage. The constitution of marriage retains a universal aspect, to be, among other things, the domestication of two parties. In this context, domestication means seclusion from the social environment to form its own entity. We see that it cannot be applicable to outside affairs, just as external social exchange cannot be applicable to domestication as a method of interaction. By default, being social is not being domesticated; it is subject to all the influence and unsettledness of worldly affairs. The moment an attempt is made to domesticate a social exchange, essentially transforming it into a familial entity, it ceases to be a social exchange in any meaningful sense. This can be understood through market exchange: the moment it is chosen to be domesticated, it is no longer available to universal market activity.

According to this premise, the government institution that provides proper social exchange would be the highest institution, since political infrastructure constitutes the most universal criteria. However, this usually does not turn out to be the case, as there are institutions that follow the marketplace itself. The marketplace is an exchange platform that supersedes political infrastructure, since it represents the sociality of biological needs. Political infrastructure does provide assistance to ensure that systems run accordingly, but the political entity is a creation of society; a complex marketplace which has evolved into a separate entity intended to oversee and administer existing subsystems and external entities.

Chapter Three: Educational Institutions

This educational institution must be perceived foremost as a political institution. We may be compelled to detach it from the political structure in which it is embedded and assume it to be merely a propagation of education itself. This is understandable, given that the constitution of the educational center is to further education. However, its constitution has no bearing under the condition of the political entity. The only variance in its particular constitution occurs when the institution has made its way into a relegated domain that is siphoned off from political proclamation. For instance, identity-bound institutions make the case for their separation from political reality and, by doing so, allow their constitution to make a mark on their setting.

However, without the control of institutions, the political reality will always be the constitution that has bearing on the institutions under its rubric. Even in the realm of the most segregated centers, it will follow that constitution; albeit with an overlay of their specific constitution. The difference is that they will enjoy a platform to interact with the political institution without being sufficiently attached to its sentiment. Whatever the psychic information of that institution, it will be endured through the observation of political reality, as is the case for highly contextualized experiences.

For example, when confined to a relationship, one may retain a high degree of conceptual engagement alongside sex-potential counterparts, but yet will receive relating material in accordance with their primal relationship. Despite the contextual separation, the reception of information will attach to the political relationship with their spouse. The difference between such a relationship and a secondary one with no contextual bearing is that the relationship material becomes embedded into the entirety of the primal relationship, which threatens to upend its stature. The same can be said for the highly contextualized educational institution, which will have its interactions embedded in political reality, albeit from an observational vantage point, without threatening the base of its primal structure.

In the case of a political institution that is unremittingly under the political apparatus, the reception of information becomes so proximate to reality that the individual is unable to interact, and thus becomes overwhelmed by its suppositions. The primal relationship, in the case of the political institution, is the homebody institution, and work hand in hand throughout the course of life.

When the political institution threatens to overwhelm the individual, for instance, in the habitat of an educational center with foreboding political influence, it weakens the child's connection to their respective homebody. They have entered an institution that can be said to wield too prosperous an influence, such that the political apparatus undermines the institution of the homebody. The problem occurs because the child requires the homebody as their base institution and, secondly, lacks the apparatus to interact with the political institution, thus becoming a puppet of its dominion. When this is the state of affairs for a developing child, they eventually become so overwhelmed by political influence, especially if it is the center of civilization, that they lose the ability to detach from that center. They are raised by the political body and know it as they would know their parents. The only personal and/or familial attachment can arrive through complete severance from the political body, through exile.

The political institution is not parent-like because it does not interact with those who interact with it. It remains stagnant in terms of personalization and cannot endow the kind of interactions expected of parental figures. The institution relies on the individual's homebody or contextual framework to engage appropriately with its substructure, and when this occurs without such mechanisms, it becomes a recipe for overwhelming influence. The political institution instead envelops the individual, for consciousness at that level will make use of whatever is placed before it, and the individual becomes a caricature of its structure. The determining factor of this character aligns with the needs of the political body, which will utilize the individual in whatever manner it sees fit. If it needs to exemplify a disparity of dissemination, it will promote individuals to represent that disparity, even at the expense of their sanity or life.

There are institutions embedded in the political spectrum but existing beyond the political sphere due to their personalized elements, which are prevalent for individual use. While regular political institutions are embedded, they often lack relevance in daily and individual use. Daily use refers to elements structurally embedded into the sequence of everyday life, something many political institutions do not possess. When detached from structural integration, an institution's significance becomes more of a conceptual notion than an existential and embodied reality. It is as if these institutions exist only as ideas, without structural evidence; and even when certainty exists, they lack daily and individual integration. Without daily use, they do not achieve structural embodiment; and without availability for citizen or individual access, they fail to integrate with social musing, leading to a loss of the conscious aspects that accompany integrated sociality.

We entertain two elements here that are closely related but worth distinguishing. The first is structural integration, not necessarily reliant on individual or citizen access. It could be sequestered from sociality yet still remain structurally embedded. This is why it's important to have political institutions that partake structurally in these networks but remain secluded from sociality, and even from the notion that sociality is in question. It may seem contradictory to be structurally embedded while adhering to a secluded sociality. Why would there need to be a structural connection if there is no social connection? However, because they gain the prerogative of structural connection, which does have social impact, it is enough to regulate their structure into something more than just an idea, thereby achieving the embodiment necessary for a realized institution.

Second, we have sociality without structural integration, which is most prevalent in forms of communication not grounded in a structural reality. While sociality can be widespread and may seem more accessible to individuals and citizens, triumphing over any structural equivalent, without structural adherence, sociality processes information through a conceptual domain rather than through embodiment. Despite appearing as emotional and existential connection, if we observe the subjective experience, it becomes clear that it is more of a conceptual interaction.

When one gains institutional or structural connections that harbor that sociality, even if the sociality itself is not structurally integrated, one gains the ability of embodiment. We see this in the educational system. Even if there is a vast structural disparity between institutions and their political entities, when the institution develops properly internally, the educational institution can become a contemplation of sociality that reaches into an embodiment by adhering to a structural connection.

To be fair, the structural connection may not exist in reality. But because sociality is genuine and available to individuals or citizens, and because it provides a structural setting that emphasizes a willingness to attach to that structural lineage, the result is a powerful experience of embodiment that comes close to a genuine structural connection. We may not find another institution that can so readily achieve structural connection without an actual structural lineage. Due to the concentrated sociality stemming from the information that ruminates within these institutions, especially considering that the information is often central to society, the result becomes an embodiment like no other.

We are reaching the great supremacy of institutions. Even if there is no structural connection, which is often the case with detachment from society, the institution can reintegrate despite its isolation. Other institutions, such as corporations, can follow a similar process, but only in the shadow of the unique benefits of educational institutions. This is why the educational system has not generally been integrated into the structural center of society like most other institutions: it already possesses the ability to gain structural lineage without securing the physical infrastructure typically necessary for structural attachment.

Even as the educational experience involves conceptual aspects, which might suggest a merely conceptual orientation, because that conceptual information is integrated into the sociality at the center of society, it moves beyond conceptuality to become general sociality. Here we have an institution that is not itself a social system, yet becomes one of the highest degrees of sociality, gaining integral embodiment despite structural detachment.[iii] From this, we can grasp that sociality itself is not the endeavor that leads to structural connection, but rather a process that makes such integration possible. As we have noted, sociality without structural integration develops to be a conceptual connection, while conceptual integration under the auspices of educational institutions becomes embodied sociality.

There we exhibit the highly prized institutions that are politically embedded, structurally integrated, and part of a circadian sociality, with access to people and citizens. Because these institutions meet all the aforementioned criteria, they are both personally relevant and politically tenable. There may be a variety of institutions under the political rubric, but only a select few receive political attention. We could say that the corporation lacks availability to the requisite individual or citizenship while being structurally connected and/or politically relevant.

Moreover, the corporation supersedes the political institution by attaining political relevance that reaches beyond its political borders. Additionally, a corporation that is structurally embedded in its suitable orientation may have a structural advantage over any political institution due to its raw power and aristocratic class, which has the ability to claim the most significant estates of structural relevance.

Political institutions counter this by utilizing political power to gain entry into such spaces, while sociality recognizes that their access was amended by state ratification, rather than arising from the true nature of sociality or economic standards. Without social recognition of that structural connection, they would lose all structural relevance. It's as if every social being that walks past the structural appropriation by the political sphere notices the gap between its fence and the fence earned by market standards, and that recognition exposes a sort of crater between the two entities.

This is why there is often a counter-reaction to politically gained structural connections, with such institutions becoming more sequestered from normal sociality or individual connection. Although it may appear that the barrier exists to protect them from external cogitation, in truth, they are positioning themselves for the same kind of social respect as any secluded space of earned structural relevance. Only, in this case it is demanded upon individual connections as if to say, "You have shut us out; we will shut you out."

Their only assurance for true appropriation is individual and social connection, leading to a reevaluation of the social approval which is typically required. These institutions rarely take such a step, because doing so would require a form self-consciousness with the acknowledgment of the political faultiness of structural appropriation as conflicting with social integration. The very fact that they have taken a reserve through political power is the very thing that they are unwilling to relinquish in order to allow individual and social connection.

This, again, is why political institutions which are structurally integrated and possess daily social use with citizens and individuals will always be among the most prevalent, comparable to corporations.

They earn their structural appropriation by participating in the daily life as well as the necessities of individual and personal access.

The Two Types of Schooling: Contextual Learning vs. Consciousness Interaction

There are two types of schooling: one that provides context and the other for a system of consciousness, or more precisely, conscious interaction. The difference between them is night and day, for conscious interaction is not concerned with context, and the very fact that schooling exists in the sense of context is merely a utility; used when needed and discarded when not. Schooling, in the word itself, such as in "schools of fish," does not refer to a contextual learning system but rather to a system of gathering for the sake of interacting for a more complex system.

Usually, when we reference a school of fish, we are discussing the less complex oceanic organisms, which "school" as a procedure to navigate the overwhelming waters, or as a form of intuitive teaching that occurs when fish partake in this communal gathering and interact with the oceanic realm. Two parameters are always present: the benefit of learning the interaction within the broader system, and the participation in a traditional framework and/or sociality that supports that. Yes, an adult fish, even a shark, might be called a school of fish, and even adults partake in this type of schooling. Corporations can be constructed in this format, acting as schooling for interaction within the conscious system. More often than not, however, they follow a different path, which is discussed in other works. Adults are less available for this type of schooling, not because they do not need it, but because they have already learned a system, making it fairly difficult to teach them a new one. When adults do enter such schooling, they may experience resentment or inability, as they have already been formatted in a different manner.

Chapter Four: The Dynamics of Hierarchical Exchange and Social Evolution

The lower end of a hierarchy, if succeeds in fulfilling its role, although vulnerable to existential (and possibly biological) ramifications, will nonetheless be able to access the entire chain of the hierarchy. Within this structure, they can exchange with each level according to that succession. They will not be hampered by the dominion of the hierarchy or the degrees of separation between levels, because by being a part of the chain, they inevitably become recipients of whatever the system has to offer. The reason for this automatic exchange is that they embody the system just as much as any other part of the organization. By that virtue, every member of the chain is required to participate in that embodiment, since the organization, or system, is a unified entity, and, more importantly, is defined by its chain of reactions.

The only concern is the potential for hampering this process of exchange, which, if left unhindered, will continue until one reaches the stage of a higher position within the hierarchy. This process may require multiple generations, as the amount of interaction necessary for such exchange can be quite elaborate. The reason each member does not ultimately become the uppermost figure in the hierarchy, namely, the leader, is less about access to exchange and more about population constraints. There can be a hindrance imposed by those at the top in an effort to control the exchange process, but that is merely an external representation. In truth, the exchange remains available to those participating at a higher level, even if not socially recognized as such.

The factors that impede this process are, for the most part, the cause of the degeneration of the organization itself, since the social reality no longer reflects its internal representation. However, over time, this dissonance will lead either to a recalibration of the system or to the complete dismantling of the organization.

Hierarchy, System Participation, and the Loss of Contrast

It is a natural occurrence that the lower end of a hierarchy will detach from the existential reality of participating in that system, since the choice is either to participate, and thus imbue the sensibility of being at the lower end of that spectrum, and threaten the biological state, as noted by multiple researchers and the health declines associated with being in the lower spectrum of a hierarchy.[iv]

This detachment does not delineate the process of being part of the system, so that in the case of non-existential participation, one will experience the full imbuement of that system as if they participate with the entirety of their psyche. In the regular case, they would simply be part of that lower spectrum but able to differentiate between that system and broader systems. But in the case of participating without the existential process, in return they will become fully embedded in that system, albeit without the degenerate experience of appearing like an inferior participant. The experience of becoming fully embedded in the system will have the individual become proficient in the enjoyment of the realities that make up that system. They will, in all respects, internalize the particulars of that system, aligning their identity, overarching sense of reality, and private life with its details.

With such a platforming of a simplistic system as being the sole generator of their psychological experience, they will lose touch with the depth of detail contained by that system and instead experience the broadness; the surface aspects. They are unable to obtain the more detailed analysis of the system because they are born within the system and have no perspective other than the system itself, such that by having no contrast they simply experience the most sentient aspects that proliferate without much interactive development, such that the flashing lights are the receptacles of that system rather than the more detailed reality of its structure. In this way, it is easy for misdirection, especially if there are structural which will imbue a sensibility that cannot be contrasted with a more in-depth analysis; much less the true nature of that system.

If such continues for a perpetual interim, they will lose more and more of the sensibility by default of having no contrast other than the system itself, such that they will rely more heavily on the objective *flashing light* without inclination or ability to provide interactive contrast. Or so, they will be completely reliant on what is most determinate as an objective experience.

Even the notion of being an objective experience, for instance, the flashing light, is also a determinately arbitrary reality, because what is objective is not so much what infuses the most attention, but rather what is socially agreed upon as determinate factors of a system. One can then lose attachment to the social agreement in favor of what is most attention-attentive to the immediate biological receptacles, whether by sight, hearing, or of libidic nature.

Even formidable constructs may be ignored from within the system despite the prevalence of social agreement pertaining to their reality. They can be forfeited for the sake of what is seemingly most attentive to the psyche, and in this way, become participants in the most relic and skeletal nature of infrastructure: that which is based on attentiveness and general social agreement, but of an infrastructural nature, not a political one.

There is another aspect of the character that shapes such an interaction, and that is the manner of approach, such that, because there is an initial unwillingness to engage with the system, the resulting experiences are defined by a resentful or negative attribution toward the system. For it is that very system that both requires of them all possibility of interaction and psychological experience, while offering them no option of participating other than becoming a representation of the lower tier of that hierarchy.. Therefore, it is not only the objective reality that is most immediate and sensible; it is the misappropriation of its construct, such that they view the *blinking light* not even as a systemic representation of shiny objects, but rather as an expression of disregard for the system all while participating in its objects; as though the commentary itself is entirely shaped by cynicism and resentment. We must iterate that it is understandable to take such an approach, because the alternatives are to be on the lower end of the spectrum and thus require, biologically, to diminish as an organism, or more so, to become subservient to the domineering effect of that hierarchy.

PART IV: LAW, EVIDENCE AND JUSTICE

Chapter One: Law, Sociality, and the Limits of Political Direction

Sociality is the furthest extent of law, and social direction is the furthest extent of political prowess. In this manner, we describe sociality as something that has been integrated into systems where only an appropriation will uncover that, in fact, it is a sociality, for instance, the notion of day or night or dressing a naked body. We would never describe clothing a naked body as a social direction or of being political, nor can we claim that day is somehow a political organization. These can be felt in nude realms, such as a bathhouse, or where nighttime develops with daytime operations, but these are only manifestations of civilization.

We would not reach the precipice of locating the realm beyond sociality, as even when we discuss organic function, it is based on a form of sociality in all that we describe, whether it is the organization of language or the imagery that gives effect to communication. Law, in its fundamental sense, is the manner of recognizing sociality, and at its most divergent points, would be considered a digression from sociality. At its most effective point, it would be the attenuation of themes of sociality that are specifically contested in other arenas, especially the political arena.

Then, as an alternative, if we have social direction, which is a force of social organization that concludes a sociality but still partakes in a specific direction, we can see the construction of a state, for example, as a political direction under the parameters of the Constitution of such a state. This is a social direction upon the regular formation of sociality, thus somewhat contesting social development or the natural social habitat.

When something is political in any of its forms of representation, whether it is personhood, identity, or conceptual construction, it will always be for a specific direction and never available to the dynamical orientation of normal sociality. This is because it already accepts sociality as a given and now proposes a direction against or for that sociality, such as security, which goes against the natural habitat of sociality and normal dynamic to impose a certain mistrust towards the possibility of that sociality. It's also because of this that it is a direction that secures elements of sociality in a specific manner, and therefore it does not follow law. If law is the exemplification of sociality, then it goes without saying that any manifestation of political orientation is against natural law. It is for this reason that the most competent state would always have a legal system that is separate from political supremacy because they naturally oppose each other and provide the necessary balance for healthy performance.

Take the example further: security goes against law because law dictates the dynamical orientation of sociality as much as it seeks to perform, which security does not allow. Now, even if we find a law in the realm of security, it is simply the restriction or imposition placed upon security as not to perform against its adequate assembly of direction so as to disrupt sociality. Meaning to say, there is no possibility of constructing law for a political system unless it is for the regulation of that social direction to not impose its criteria beyond its means. Therefore, it attempts to find security to give it a certain definition but only as the law allows political supremacy to be given the 'right.'

Rights are the political supremacy. Thus, saying, "We give you a right to do such and such," despite the fact that sociality is in blatant disagreement with such or in how law manifests itself in opposition. One does not have a right to walk upon the street, for that is a social manifestation, but they do have a right of passage. We do not need the right of way when sociality progresses to the point where it is simply understood unto which criteria should be given at that intersection. The right of way is only a political imposition to avoid the confusion for which sociality has not progressed towards.

In the contemporary era, in which sociality has gained momentum, it is a difficult process to discern the levels of attainment of sociality which do not even have the imprint of political direction. Such is the waiting ground for the occurrence, sometimes without any definition, agreement, or awareness, since one would have to understand all of history, especially the history of civilization, to acknowledge all the attainment of sociality henceforth and to find its elements within the system.

The nature of sociality is that it does not have a political direction nor a political representation. Thus, it performs itself by its internal credence, which cannot be explored, understood, or regulated. The credence is the basis of a former political orientation or representation, which is now superseded to become a full form sociality. To grant the sociality its former political head as a political representation will retrogress the entire format of sociality to its antiquated form. Sociality itself has a choice to go in the direction it sees fit and may even go back to its earlier frameworks, which may seem to present itself as a political direction.

The highest form of law is that which manifests from the most developed criteria of sociality in all its manifestations. This reflects the intricate structure of sociality, by the distinct development of each individual and their participation in various organizational forms. Consequently, what emerges is not merely the sociality of the majority, as it might be construed from a political standpoint, but rather sociality in its most genuine and comprehensive form. Its marginalized elements are noticed as a minority, not because it is a minority opinion, but rather because it has not presented itself to the full form of sociality as is deemed fit and/or granted recognition.

Whenever an organization has the fortitude to manifest a representational head of a developed sociality, for example, when it was representatively relevant to teach the notion of clothing naked persons, it is for a political benefit and thus politically contracted. It is a direction of sociality against current sociality, which already thinks of itself as understandable to that criteria, so that the only matter of enriching that original representation is through a specific social direction, which always makes it political. This is not to say that it's not necessary to have that representational element, but sociality alone, by itself, becomes a lacking substrate without its original form. It is a political reality that one must answer to in order to gain that axis. However, to enter that political arena, say, for the representational element of clothing nakedness, it must be performed so that it does not lose the current sociality, for then all of that development is circumvented for the purpose of its original sentiment.

Law cannot assist in this regard, for the law that manifests from sociality can dictate to the criteria of dressing nakedness in private or public but cannot dictate how it came about or why such a thing is purposeful. But at the same time, law does provide the nuanced capability of the social concept of clothing nakedness so that it is now part of a lawful discourse that aligns as much as possible with current sociality. It is still a social concept and not sociality itself, and there will be a buffer between the two, though law's purpose is to align as closely as possible with true and concurrent sociality. When law deviates from either genuine sociality or from a specific social purpose like political objectives, then it becomes outside the realm of law and is rather considered statutes for political use or a credence for social use; it is not law in the sense of justice and its complex system. This is why the competent practice of law must always align with the cities of that state or sociality, so that they can obtain an alignment to a sufficient degree so it is not to base their criteria upon logic, rationality, or specific social purpose. In this sense, law is not social, but it is a form of sociality.

Hart (2006) suggests, "...One of the constitutive elements of the complex social practice that comprises a legal system, and, more particularly, to specify that element which permits us to say that law is not just a social practice, but a normative social practice...."[v]

What is missing from the proprietorship of law is that it manifests a social normality which does not requisite its very normative structure. Law simply is the inheritance of sociality as it would constitute a social concept when there is a disputation of that criteria. We could dictate that there is a whole book of law that has not yet written but is supposed by current sociality, yet because there is no opposition or intersection to which a proclamation is needed, it is not recognized as a social concept in its judicial form. Law can be constituted as a normative social practice, but in reality, it is a normative exemplification of social concepts that mostly align with current sociality, to which it is not the genuine makeup of any social hierarchy. It is the discourse that must be had, despite the prevailing possibility of building a conglomerate of current sociality for its dynamic and constant motion. Besides the fact that it would be near impossible to pinpoint its stature, the law requires a weighty deliberation of this course to ensure that it is most aligned with general sociality or non-marginalized sociality.

In this analysis, we could constitute judiciaries not as representatives of the public from a political perspective, but rather as a manner of exemplification for social recognition, not to represent sociality, but to align with it. The practical ramifications would be that the law system remains transitory while the political system stagnates. This is the veneration offered to a judge, similar to that of royalty offered to a political figure. The honor of the judge is due of the honor of oneself, and the notion of honor and/or shame is closely attributed to familial systems, as well as internal systems.

Hart (2006) notes, "Habits and rules both involve regular patterns of behavior, but rules also involve, and are partly constituted by, a characteristic normative attitude: Those who accept the rule regard the pattern of behavior as a common and binding standard of conduct."[vi] Hart further dictates that laws are a binding standard of conduct, to which it would seem that sociality is requesting standardization, or that the political forum is declaring such recognition. We would assert that it is rather from a third place, the standard that requires it to be a standard because sociality is not given its peculiar credence of merit.

In this case, the functional society requires less standardization of conduct or law because sociality itself, in each citizen's recognition of it and its moving parts, will constitute its structure, so that few intersections or contestations are made possible. We find prevailing law where the standard of conduct is suboptimal, such that we need to create a synchronized version, which is a certain deviation from sociality because it is a statute of text that pertains to a very specific amelioration, one which is based on an analysis rather than concurrent sociality. One can find that in the change of a season, sociality has already evolved to a place where it would not constitute the same standard of conduct. Rather, law cannot follow at such a nuanced level, such that a subgroup of society will gain prominence, while others will either follow the standard of law as dictated by social professionals or by law itself.

Before an alignment of law is processed, there is the cause of the social professional, or one who perceives and processes sociality in a manner that can be dictated in a dialogical format, to which law then proceeds to have as its preliminary draft. If we follow any draft of law, we can find its preliminary stages in social professionals who have built the criteria to which law now processes via a more complex format. It is possible for there to be a population in the interior of sociality that presupposes its very structure by their adherence to social professionals, such that they may be following and assuming the sociality of a decade or two prior. In this case, they either demand or partake in current sociality with that perspective.

Social professionals begin their analysis either by simply taking account of sociality, not for the sake of opposition or intersection, but merely as an appropriation of sociality. This form of discourse can then, in effect, form a criteria for intersection or opposition, to which a standard of law must be enacted. It is as if one arrives to the table bearing an analysis, to which the rest are simply a dynamic reflection of that. This now creates a form of contestation which thus requires a standard of law. By simply bearing the current discourse of sociality, it thus opens the box to intersection which was not present before. There is the kind of intersection that simply occurs, like a road crossing with its right of way, to which the intersection is simply the mechanism of vehicle and pedestrian procedure. The intersection is the enacted experience of confusion or frustration between sociality and not a social discourse that brought about this opposition.

Domestic law becomes an interesting subject, and disregard for the intersection of sociality never occurs since it is not a public arena. When we do not have sociality, we cannot provide an exemplification of sociality, such that domestic law is a contradiction in terms. If we follow the discourse of domestic law, we notice that it first formats as a political direction; a political stance focused on private affairs, such that a specific social direction is seeking a constitution of law. This process brings to bear an array of domesticated elements as if they were a public notation, which then enacts a codex of law.

It remains, at all times, a political process, for the instant the political discourse does not recognize domestication or its process, and it reverts into the domesticated arena, away from sociality. Even with the most extreme of domesticated elements, such as homicide in the private sphere, such would be a public form of sociality which entreaties retribution. That is, unless there is a manner to which that domesticated sphere intersects with the public in a way that has social recognition, but without, the retribution is not a social element but rather a regulated political stance.

The political organization recognizes this homicide within domesticated affairs to be either a public nuance or a problem for a variety of reasons. Because sociality does not inherit or recognize domesticated hitches which may ascend, this does not mean there are no vulnerabilities. A homicide within domesticated affairs will naturally produce a later social disparity, and thus the political organization recognizes such a takes premeditated action. However, if one considers the comparison of homicide recognized in the public arena, or instances where domestication intersects with the public, then, if the familial body has a representative element participating in sociality, it becomes an entirely different matter of judgment, as sociality itself assumes the precedent, independent of political intervention.

The more private the sphere of influence, the less impactful it would be to sociality, and thus to the precedent of law. Alternatively, the more public the sphere, whether it is a domestic product or a communal one, the more it would establish precedent for law to proceed alongside political action.

Political action itself does not necessarily constitute a superior organization but can be a domesticated form of political action. For example, a nomadic institutional structure offers political action to a private sector, whether it is family units, heads of families, or neighborhood organizations, to which the social direction is implied by the populace, despite the very fact that it is a domesticated structure from top to bottom.

Political action in this regard is an anomaly, for the admixture of domesticated elements and social direction disrupts both dominions, such that it cannot be constituted as a private affair. Although any group or social function can choose a social direction, it turn out to be a political process. From that outset, it does not recognize its domesticated elements in relation to a broader sociality not included in the representation of this smaller format of political concern. This creates a social-political function that does not understand broader society to which it is in opposition or indirect opposition, thus belligerent to an invisible enemy. The entire structure of the domesticated process does not understand this minor form of political direction because it is merely a proprietary notion of something much more complex, which is disruptive and troublesome to understand or else to perform the objective it seeks.

The experience of disruption in these private affairs is troublesome, to which a minor form of a political organization is a natural response, much like a parent to a household. When there is confusion, parents seek to direct their power in a differing manner against the sociality of the natural family body. But they do so without recognizing that the entire structure of the family body is simply the domesticated elements of a larger sociality, and that the impulsive political organization at the lower level does not constitute the response to the problem which has arisen.

Political function can only be recognized as a social direction to a specific form of sociality, yet the sociality must itself be incorporated into the political direction, additionally, this must be the criteria of the political direction by understanding that sociality. If either of these is untrue, if the social direction is a misunderstanding of the criteria of sociality, like the head of the household or the nomadic tribe, or if sociality itself does not accept the social direction or the political legitimacy as a whole, it is simply the dealings of an imposition and will not be organized as a specific direction to which sociality must adhere.

Let us discuss the element of sociality accepting the legitimacy of the political function or its social direction. We do not mean the arbitrary acceptance of individuals or impositions, but rather sociality as it is familiarized, whether individually or communally, such that there is the possibility of acceptance because an intersection exists between these two bodies. A marginalized sociality, however, can reflect a lack of acceptance as if it is a misalignment when, in fact, there is none. If a majority simply asserts that it rejects a political or social direction, such does not translate to a misalignment, especially since it is pronounced. It is but a marginalized element of sociality, for sociality itself is an amelioration of its dynamic force and does not adhere to the nuanced proclamations of its substructure. By virtue of being a demonstrated element or proclamation, it performs itself as marginalized, like one standing up and saying, "This is sociality," when it is simply a dynamic force changing with every moment.

One might be confused by this analysis and assume sociality can never proclaim itself, and this is true, for the mere act of demonstration disrupts the normative function of sociality and performs as a political function, as one political function disagreeing with another. It is as if two opposing political functions are in opposition while normative sociality continues unabated, almost as if it were a marginalized element among the sphere of combatants.

As noted before, if law follows a social direction instead of sociality itself, it becomes a political organization rather than a social one. Though the legislative element of law may seem to follow a discourse of public concern, it is instead responding to proclamations of a marginalized element of the public, thereby constituting a political organization. It is as if a state within a state requests the legislative body to intercede and perform its legislative function. Besides law using its legislative power to perform a political function, it also grants credence to a fringe political body against the hierarchy of the greater political institution that intersects at a more potent level per current sociality. This is disruptive, not only in performing as a legislative body rather than a political one, but also in legitimizing a fringe state contestation against the majority state.

Chapter Two: The Charitable Balance of Private and Public Law

Law is based on a construct that offers the most charitable solution for a qualitative function. For instance, law states that property is private to the beholder, despite ownership being part and parcel of all society; for if the boat is part of a market, then it is part of a market share, and without that market, it would not be considered valued property. Because of this, it is offered to the beholder of property to take full control of its domain and constitute it as private.[vii]

Although this relieves ownership away from the market or from the public itself, it is most charitable in that each person has rights to the experience of privacy in their domain, so long as they have a domain, so that when they are out and about, they cannot claim ownership of another's private domain, thus balancing that forfeiture.

We could say the opposite is occurring, but then in the public domain, the law will be on the side of the general public even when it contrasts certain private accessibilities, so that we are offering a public experience in contrast to a certain private ownership pertaining every citizen of that city or state. It is most charitable this way because the constituents would be considered rather for the allowance of having access to a public domain as such, and to forfeit that little semblance of private access that is their own from the public process.[viii]

Chapter Three: The Ownership Ideal: Between Interaction and Political Proclamation

Internal ownership is that in which the source and dependency are in applied synchronization. This differs from external ownership, wherein the dependency is proposed as a dependency, in which the source does not apply psychic attachment for its innate material but rather from its notion of ownership. One is behooved to the ideal of ownership, which can be the political reality, or even social reality; such is the ideal of that synchronization. For instance, the political entity may ascertain that a deed of a property is constituted as ownership, while the individual does not experience a psychic delineation in regard to said property. The ownership is an ideal, whereas there is no psychological attachment other than the notion of that ideal. Meaning to say, the psychological attachment is in relation to one's attachment to the political association rather than the property itself.

Even more dramatic is the case of a child's dependency, if the "ownership" is based on an ideal of responsibility, constituted by both social norms as well as political concern, then the psychological attachment to the child is only in consideration of the political and social entity. When the case brings a detachment from both the political and social entity, the attachment to the child will dwindle alongside that. In a very real sense, the ownership is one of participation in the sociality which constituted that ideal.

When we view the autonomous nature of one's body, we notice the same pattern. While most would view their body as a form of ownership of some kind, it can be the case where such is constituted as an ideal rather than internal ownership. The ideal of one's body as their own must be a derivative of some form of society, whether political or social norm, to which that attachment will wane in the case of detachment from both. We do not have to look far for evidence of this, wherein the outsider or the one living detached from civilization, noticed in the many series that follow the day-to-day of their activity, a very direct correlation takes place. Each constituent will begin to detach from the political and social reality from which they arrived, and in that case, their attachment to selfhood and its biological entity diminishes alongside that. They do not lose all sense of their ownership of their selfhood, but only the external form, so that all excess will be diminished.

Their body, instead of bearing the political or social associations, takes a view of how their internal mechanism perceives the ordeal. Of course, that internal realm is based on the very interactions that were constituted in the social and political realm, but being a manifestation of internal reserve, they resolve themselves in accordance with genuine ownership. In that case, they do experience such ownership of the body not as a notion or ideal but rather as a dynamic to that perspective, where they interact with that dependency.

Thus, internal ownership is really another way of phrasing interaction between selfhood and dependencies. If one chooses to interact with a tree, viewing the tree in proportion to some aspect of themselves, they will gain a certain sense of ownership. If the next moment they find the tree to be no longer there, it will arouse an emotion akin to that of their own demise, ever since it has become part of their existence. Although the political and social entity will not agree with the premise that every interaction constitutes a proprietorship, the psychological reality is that one becomes engaged in a possession with all that they interact with, so long as it is considered a real interaction.

This is why public transport is so dramatic to the social, political, and individual realm, since it is bound with the internal ownership of all its users, all the while with a political proclamation of ownership, and still more, with a social version of that. Thereby, each cubit of public transport is owned by three parties: the political entity, the general social entity, and every constituent who interacted with that cubit of space.

We do see compensation for this conflict, whereas the political entity applies a very broad consensus of its ownership to include and not limit any and all users, while the general sociality will view its ownership in the amalgamation of each individual and their sense of internal or external ownership. And finally the individual will allow for the premise of the political consensus by viewing their ownership as part and parcel of that social statement.

For illustration, if one experiences trauma en-route, which is a dramatic imprint of their ownership to that space or aspect, they will neglect to include the ownership of all other parties. This neglect of inclusion will be a state of conflict for the other parties who seek their experience of ownership, and at its extreme, will have the political entity intercede, or that of the social realm to balance that ownership. In the case of the political entity staking too much ownership, it will either have the practice of utility decline or have the constituents ascertain to the political attachment rather than personal interaction. This will have the ownership manifest into an ideal rather than internal ownership, where the political entity and its proclamations will be the manner of interaction for all the experience of that public transport. This very idea is the cause of contention between all parties, so that any inclination toward one over the other will constitute a dramatic imbalance of a succeeding society.

We could view the ideal of ownership, or external ownership, as the prerequisite for internal ownership, which the political entity proposes as the ideal, which then has the individual find a personal regard to that ownership. This would mean that any internal interaction is based on an ideal of interaction or ownership.

Let us take the case of the tree: what constitutes the individual to interact with the tree? Does the political entity take an idealized view of the ownership towards trees or that of nature? We can view this in a scalable manner, where the political entity does constitute the notion of ownership towards property or possessions, and any and all that fit that criteria will be enabled to gain private ownership. In the case of a tree, since the individual has followed the ideal of the political entity in regards to property, the tree is possible to remain in that parameter and thus gain private ownership.

This would mean that in the nomadic tribes of antiquity, wherein the political entity was fairly moderated, and constitutions of property were more arbitrary, the individual interactions toward entities would also be absent. This does explain how those societies were mostly preoccupied with direct social interactions, focused on tribes and their internal sociality rather than tools, objects, possessions, and property. Nomadic is their constitution; thus, mobility was not viewed as a chance from one property to another but rather a state of affairs where social interactions were the only merit of interaction. (Levi-Strauss, Tristes Tropiques) (Freud, Civilization and Its Discontents) (Anthony Smith, The Ethnic Origin of Nations, 1996.)[ix, x, xi]

With some hesitation we conclude the dilemma that the ideal of property is the precursor for an individual sense of interaction, such that one will protect their body and autonomy because the social and political entity regarded it as such. We must agree to such because the opposite is true, wherein the political and social entity retains the dexterity to have the individual lose protection of an individual body and/or autonomy. This offers an addition to our understanding of the modern suicidal and drug problem, whereas it might be the constitution of the political or social aspect which allows and proclaims to the effect of following such a path. Despite the clear indication of a contrary position, we find a very empathetic notion toward the ordeal such that an individual will receive that position as a proclamation of ideals, to the point where personal protection will dissipate to make available to the political sentiment. This is the warry sign of political empathy, which will be received contrary to its supposition by a portion of the citizen base.

If we are to conclude that the political and social entity can remove protection of one's life, then we can derive the fact that the entire premise of self-protection is an ideal of those entities. This can be extended to where the private realm can interact with that sentiment, such that it becomes a private ownership of their bodily entity. This is only after the fact, where the individual has incorporated the external ideal, to the point where they view ownership of the body with such legitimacy that it would seems as an individual conclusive process, and this point of research seems almost a stretch of the imagination.

The Dynamics of Ownership

The switch between internal ownership and external ownership can occur rapidly, with either the ideal preceding the internal interaction, or the internal interaction receding to the ideal. Take the example of one's family body, which usually begins from an ideal, with the insulation of marriage or at least the political recognition of the family body. That ideal then reaches a plateau where there is internal interaction among its constituents.

The holiday, for instance, is found in the developed family body because they have formalized that ideal to the point of internal reciprocity. The beginning stages do not have the time to incorporate the external ideal and thus are more prone to participate in another more developed family for holidays. However, the later stages of a family body recede back into the ideal, either because they have diminished in size or because the formalization of interactions has been exacerbated to a point where they are on the lookout for an ideal to be incorporated. If the argument is only to the effect of a change of generation, there is ample evidence to the contrary in the case of renowned, famed, royal, affluent family bodies, where the change of generation does not exhaust the interactions within that domain. This is because they have incorporated the ideal by virtue of their very attachment to the social and political realms. They do not exhaust, as in the regular case, because of their continuing participation in the ideal, which can be possible for any citizen but is made completely accessible by the social demand of their participation, which is not the case for the regular citizen.

One can enter into the ideal of ownership when they neglect or overlook the interactive elements, contrary to the regular case of mere interactive exhaustion. For example, the case of trauma would have one divert attention away from the interactive material pertaining to the trauma, to the amicable state of continuing their psychological state without the burden of those interactions. In that case, they will proceed from the traumatic instance into the ideal state of ownership pertaining to the associations of the trauma. If the trauma is related to authority figures, a specific location, or any other aspect of association, they will relate to those aspects in accordance with their ideal. If it is a specific location, then any interactions with that location will not be internal, but rather based on the ideal of participating in that location and claiming ownership of that realm. If the case is an authority figure, then all authority figures will be viewed in the ideal of authority rather than the internalized state of authority. They will become enmeshed in these ideals, proclaiming ownership for the psyche, all without interaction with the constitutions of these ideals. They will lose perspective on the interactions regarding authority or that location and instead will participate in the notion of authority, or in the symbolic nature of that location. This is the manner in which a state can decline, when its citizens follow the symbolic nature of the state, or the ideal of the state, to which there is little to no interaction based on the state, since an ideal is not an interaction but the ideal of an interaction.

There is a circumstance in which internal ownership is not only a practical notion but is a necessity for the manner of the environment. In the case where there is general sociality that concludes or precludes a determination toward universal ownership, despite the political accession which dictates property limits or ritual proclamations of property parameters, still, it will be the case that the social realm concludes that there is no separation of property or individuality. This is the usual case in competent realms where the political aspect has less influence because general sociality has determined that it reaches all its crevices, so that the political statement does not have power to separate those divisions.

When we discuss political power, we refer in the case of a psychological experience, such that even as the political sentiment is a separation of property, the psychological state will not be constituted as such. For example, a train within city limits constitutes a general sociality that overrides the political statement, and subsequently general sociality asserts universal ownership, with no separation between locations or stops, while the political assertion maintains a format to each part of its line. Therefore, the psychological state of individuals using that mode of transport would be one of continuous experience flanked by its realms, despite political separation and even infrastructural separations like doorways or stops, since general sociality overrides all of that.

The reason general sociality overrides political sentiment is that the latter is a representation of the former, and a source of representation will be more present than the representational effect of political attributes. The individual is bound to general sociality because they derive much of their perception from the affordances of that entity. A train, for instance, is viewed as a direct connection between parts of town, rather than as distinct localities with an arbitrary bridge between them. Sociality would dictate otherwise because it follows the amalgamation of all sociality, which, when combined, having all continuities connect to various parts in no distinct manner, concludes that the entire sphere is one giant connective tissue.

This is untrue structurally, as each door, each building, and each movement is distinct. Individually, it is only based on specific interactions according to individuality and ownership. The only method of separating general sociality from internal ownership is when the ownership manifests in a directive manner toward the element that constitutes the private interaction. Despite sociality dictating no separation between spaces, if one asserts a separation, at least psychologically, they will notice structural separation. However, within those parameters, they must interact with that ownership in an internal sense, such that it is not a political or social assertion that would defeat the objective.

Once those entities are introduced, one would not gain the sought-after separation because general sociality overrides whatever premise they have decided. The only case of separation is through both individual ownership in a psychological sense, and the interactions that make that possible, where it is now considered, at least psychologically, their own realm, despite the disagreement of general sociality. The reason general sociality does not override one's internal ownership is that the internal process is not reliant on external perception or a dependency on sociality; it is truly private to one's domain.

If we think of the concept of ownership itself, it can be understood as a modality that precedes perception. The perceptual realm cannot entertain ownership because it must follow whatever it perceives and, in some way, is owned by the forms that are offered to perception. However, when ownership exists, it makes itself available for direct experience despite the prevailing format of perception. Its adage might be something like this: "Whatever the perceptual realm, this ownership will not be distracted by it." Contestation of ownership occurs when something from the perceptual realm disrupts that private experience of attachment, such as war or natural disaster, which removes much of the ownership, whether property or possession, merely because it acts as an entranceway from perception to those realms.

Chapter Four: Evidential and Non-Evidential: A Dual Framework of Reality

Evidence is evidential, and therefore its primary attribute is how it presents itself, with seemingly little to no associations, especially those of subjective nature. That very attribute is its vulnerability, since it is evidential by a single criterion but non-evidential by every other possible criterion. Something that would constitute as evidential might be structural habitats or objects of reality. For these, because their evidential aspect is shape and size without much negotiation of their presence, they delineate all possibilities that are not of such character. It is not evidential to an all-encompassing criterion because of its evidential status. Rather it has a direction toward all perspectives that may be reached, disallowing a perspective from reaching any other endpoint.

In all our analysis, we must reach the object of inquiry at its fundamental aspect, so that it is both fundamental as a single criterion and fundamental as being elementary to all-encompassing perspectives. Even the wording of fundamentality is constituted with both positive and negative attributes, a fundamentalist, for instance, or fundamentality. The negative attribute is how an object does not allow for delineation, while the positive attribute is in how it does have a very real quality that is not available for negotiation.

Non-evidential objects, systems, or constructs are embedded with the possibility of a very large degree of nuance and variability. Their vulnerability s that they do not contain an objective, evidential point to which all perspectives culminate. They can follow a range of perspectives without ever reaching an endpoint that performs any substantiation. An example of a non-evidential system would be a

Constitution or the construct of a state, which, although associated with evidence for its substantiation, is merely the performance of its range of perspectives. It is for this very reason that a state must represent itself; without it, would not be evidential.

When we discuss how evidence is a dominant participant in any discussion or negotiation, we are merely discussing the very fact that there is not a culminating endpoint. Evidence in a courtroom, while gaining very strict parameters about what is being discussed, is open to any perspective until that endpoint is reached. A contemporary example would be evidence in the form of picture or film, which, although carrying substantiation of an endpoint, every photographer would admit does not culminate in a singular point of succession. It is not merely disagreement about the reality of a photograph or video, which is socially acceptable as some form of substantiation, but rather that it does not reach an evidential endpoint to which discussion of a single photograph or film would not reach the same social conclusion, as would a perceptual experience.

Non-evidential aspects are not to be considered lesser than evidential; for them, there is the possibility of perspectives that do not require the rigid conclusion that an evidential aspect demands. As we have noted, very powerful non-evidential constructs are part of social and psychological systems, for instance, the Constitution of a family body, or the proliferation of a state. Likewise, evidential aspects that are not themes are more noteworthy, for example, simplistic infrastructure such as rocks or trees, which are evidential but provide no nuance or strong adaptation for social process or psychological development.

For this very reason, and due to its dichotomy, one would need to relinquish evidential aspects to allow for perspectives in the non-evidential arena. Likewise, one must admit or accept a non-evidential reality alongside a proposed evidential one, so as to avoid the demanding conclusion that the evidential aspect requires.

Chapter Five: Three Layers of Truth: On Psyche, Structure, and Evidentiary Reality

There are three levels of truth or forms of reality in regard to evidential reality. The first and foremost level, which can be deemed a continental truth, is that of a core functionality of one's system.

[1] This primary level of truth is fundamental, and therefore any assertions must acquiesce to its fundamentality. For example, it is a fundamental truth that sexuality is a characteristic of one's internal system and thus public sociality, but more so, that it must embody a characteristic that provides a role in opposition to another role, intertwined in a dynamic fashion. Why this is a truth is less important than dealing with that fundamentality.

If one were to assert zero ascendancy of sexuality, more so than simply dismissing the fundamentality, they would be embodying it in a different format. In some sense, they would be energizing the very proposition of zero ascendancy by sublimating an experienced aspect of sexuality, such that the driving force of this form of non-sexuality is sexuality. If one were to assert that there is a single characteristic to embody the form of sexuality, they would be associated with the opposing characteristic, because one requires the reflection of the experiential self by virtue of needing something beyond their subjective experience. If one were to serve a new form that is not in proposition to this dynamic, it would, in its fundamental sense, embedded within these two opposing characteristics for the reason that they embody the form of sexuality.

Another example would be the parent–child relationship: when a child asserts autonomy, this act does not negate their parental lineage but instead affirms it, often more deeply than passive agreement would. In exercising independence, they enact the developmental trajectory embedded in that lineage. The fundamentality of their parental connection and its dependency is not terminated by the psyche and therefore will register as a reversal. The same is true for one who primarily views their identity among their parents'; they will express a finite and distinct mode of interacting with that parental figure, thereby enacting contrary to that supposition and being distinct even as they appear similar. The fundamental truth is embedded in the system such that, wherever one chooses to go, they encounter it.

The reason these are considered fundamental truths is that they are a basis of the system of affairs in which the psyche participates, and of the negotiation possible for the psyche. For example, individuality versus communal, central localities versus marginalized localities, prominent figures versus citizens, these fundamental realities are molded into the psyche and are part of the system, one which does not have a degree in which it can be changed through intellectual manipulation.

For example, virtue will always be individualistic in comparison to the communal sphere; if one pushes to the extreme by asserting the individual state as the quintessential modality of being, they will manifest strong elements of the communal form; possibly more so than if they agreed to that dichotomy. The reason it is a fundamental truth is because of the perceptual mode of the psyche and the internal mode, such that there will always be a separation between the individual and the external sphere, which affords each other in a mutually exclusive fashion.

In the centric locality, it is the fundamental reality that a central part of a sphere participates in all the ongoing processes of marginalized aspects, such that marginalized aspects are in complete dependence on the central process. This applies to location, geography, and geopolitics. It is not fundamentally possible to negotiate such a process, but only to determine in what way one meets aspects relegated by that spectrum. There is no process in which one acts upon marginalized aspects of a central location and reaches self-sufficiency; just like the individual endeavoring comprehensive individuality will merely express strong aspects of the communal sphere.

The same applies to a prominent figure versus a regular citizen; in that dichotomy of social differentiation, there is no possibility to negotiate the spectrum, but only juncture contained by that spectrum. We can never dictate that the regular citizen is complete prominence, nor that the prominent figure is in complete embodiment of the regular citizen; rather, there is negotiation between these two fundamental exchanges.

By the fact that we have mentioned multiple examples of this process for what constitutes a fundamental truth, it might seem that one should cancel the other. If we dictate that it is a fundamental truth afforded to the dichotomy of individuality and communal aspects, it should be the case that central locations differ on a range from marginalized locations, because these are two different spectrums and we are asserting singular fundamental truths. This may be so, but such fundamental truths partake in all processes of life, such that at any point in time, one is either a citizen or a prominent figure, individualized or participating in the communal sphere, contained by marginalized territory or a central location, and so on. At no point is the individual outside of this, despite the multitude of spectrums.

[2] This would be the general consensus; however, if we inquire further than the fundamental truth, the difference between evidential and non-evidential is based on a concluding endpoint that is objective according to a certain criteria. If that were the case, even a construct could be considered evidential by virtue of the conclusive endpoints being as the proliferation and acceptance of the stature of a state, despite its modality being conceptual.

In this case, a construct is not considered outside the realm of evidence because there is a conclusive endpoint. However, it remains a construct because it is not substantiated by a direct correlation to infrastructure and the objective status of the external realm. Further, if there is an inconclusive consensus of an external object, it may be possible to conclude it is a non-evidentiary object.

If all sociality agrees that a box in its external form is not constituted as a box or an object, it remains inconclusive as an object and therefore would be constituted as non-evidentiary. However, the very modality of having social parties provide a conclusive consensus of its inconclusivity means sociality does in fact agree to its conclusive nature. It would only be in the case where differing points of view show indifference to the object as it constitutes itself as an object, to then be considered a non-evidentiary object.

If the social realm commissions a psychological reversal, it would not be considered evidence; just as if all agree that the weather is cloudy when it is in fact sunny, it would be an attempt to be inconclusive, all the while embedded in the psyches of each participant is conclusivity, even as it is being proposed as inconclusive. An example of an object finding difference is the case of an object in a simulation, such as a video game, where the social realm conclusively agrees that such an object is in fact an object, but in no way is based on a proposition of inconclusivity but rather indifference, as if there is no question to be asked; such that if it were asked it would be inconclusive as an object.

We could take this further in questionable simulatory systems, such as museums or highly interactive environments, which follow some components of stimulatory nature and attempt to assimilate various frameworks of minds, all while being simple structures in response to the contemporary era. An object in such a simulation could be inconclusive as a real object, especially those that attempt to offer a simulatory framework, such as an art piece.

If we can conjure a general social agreement that the entire experience of life is simulatory to a point where there is indifference to the objects, such that it would be inconclusive based on that indifference, then we have reached a plethora of objects that would constitute as non-evidentiary external objects. However, such is not the case, and therefore external objects are readily concluded as conclusive and thus evidentiary.

The problem with a conclusive criterion is that its outcome is already generated before the interaction occurs. The object is thus an object for the psyche before ever having the possibility of deciding it is an actual object. Of course, there is a preliminary context based on the development of the psyche which correlates to the fact that it is an object, but because of its evidentiary status and the conclusive attributes, it does not have any ability to destabilize to a point where a new perspective is possible.

[3] Conclusivity is where there is a multitude of authentication points, which by their very differentiation create general agreement that what is being perceived is evidentiary. The authentication pathways must be differentiated from each other or it would be considered a single authentication pathway; its entire purpose is to differentiate until the impact of outcome. There is a convergence with the authentication points, and this is the most vulnerable part of the evidentiary outcome, because it must create a consensus at some point that the authentication points correlate without the pathways themselves correlating. If the pathways correlate, then it is not a differentiated authentication point; if they do not eventually converge, then there is no single outcome to produce an evidentiary statement.

This juncture of convergence between authentication pathways is made possible by an agreement hosted by a novel platform. The reason is that if any authentication pathway offered itself as the converging platform, it would be partialized based on its pathway and thus disrupt the convergence from being solely based on an endpoint convergence. This novel platform, for example, an object in the environment, would be conducted by an aspect of the psyche that agrees with itself but does not do more than itself nor correlate to other parts of the psyche. It is true to itself; thus, we have statements when experiences are very dramatic, where people say, "I cannot believe it," or "It is really happening," or "This is beyond apprehension." These correlate to the modality of the psyche that stands by itself without correlating to the authentication pathways, allowing the premise that it alone is the formidable truth, not because of itself, but because the convergence of the multitude of pathways has rested upon it.

The validity of a single authentication pathway is based on a preliminary track record of its evidentiary outcomes. Meaning, we trust vision more than auditory because of the realization that what has been brought to sight has reached an evidentiary marker or outcome that succeeds what was brought to audible attention. We measure this by the correlation of movement in evidentiary aspects; if we see a conclusive ideation that links to other external events and retains continuous ideation, then it is considered authentic.

For example, if we hear a noise but do not see its outcome, or see a different outcome than the presupposed notion of that noise, we conclude that the auditory pathway is less conclusive than vision. To prove the validity of an authentic pathway is by correlating itself with how a sequence of events changes in respect to the external sphere. It is possible that one interprets the sequence of events according to the preliminary authentication pathway, manipulating external movement as a measure to purport evidence for their authentic pathway. This is corrected by a continuous cycle where the authentication pathway proceeds based on its supposition to correlate with the sequence of events in such a pattern and motion that eventually there is no ability to reinterpret changes other than through its authentication process.

Vision is given a higher authentication gradation than auditory because of the continuous cycles between what sight offers as conciliatory perception and external sequence of events. When we see an object constituted as an object that fits the profile in the sequence of events, and this process recurs moment to moment, it justifies the authentication pathway of vision as higher than that of audio. When we hear something and then follow the sequence of events, if the outcome is different because audio has more difficulty with conclusivity, it offers a lower gradation of authentication. However, each authentication pathway may offer unique characteristics that can offer differing directions to the evidentiary outcome. In order to achieve evidentiary standards at the time of convergence, negotiation and procedure of the authentication pathways are required.

Part V: Politics and Consciousness

Chapter One: The Encapsulation of Consciousness: A Reflection on Historical Vantage Points

Conscious experience is genuinely a generic or wholesome process in single continuous flow, akin to wind or other unified natural elements. There are an infinite number of vantage points within that encapsulation, which does have a parameter for evolution. For instance, the conscious unveiling of the sanctimonious nature of life and death was finalized, to a certain extent, by the Egyptians and was then taken too far and mediated throughout the coming of ages. However, the specific conscious relevance has been uncovered and now can never be put back into its casing. Still, there are a vast number of vantage points through which to perceive that sacrificial understanding, all of which are true in their final access to that consciousness.

Therefore, although there are major junctures that define consciousness, such as the year marker or the century marker, these are only methods of accessing a specific point of consciousness. Any others can be just as valid for the process. The purpose is to understand that an encapsulation of consciousness, and some political sentiment carries such along, which may even seem to perpetuate activity, leading one to assume that it now defines consciousness. It is no wonder that history books are primarily filled with differing battles and this will likely remain true for the future.

If we consider the World War II era, it is finalized as the pre-war and post-war era, despite whatever cultural relevance may seem pressing. Of course, we now have catalogs of data if one is interested in, for instance, examining the film industry, art, fashion, or any other reference point. Just as we cannot fully view 1843s' art culture, fashion, real estate, or economy, we could, however, view the 1840s decade in respect to those aspects. Still, some things remain anchored in discordant political change.

Now, if we were to go further back, say, to the 1600s, we could not easily provide an account of the 1620s in terms of fashion, art, or other forms, but only political sentiment. Technically we could, through research, but it's usually only when art enters the political sphere, such as in response to the church during the Renaissance. We could not describe the specific dress of the 1620s, though research could uncover that, albeit with little immediate relevance.

If we go to the height of the Roman Empire, we are genuinely bound to the century and mostly to political aspects. Although we could observe gradual cultural change, we do not usually account for it as a general acceptance of Roman culture, even though it is, nonetheless, true. For instance, Roman fashion featured one shoulder bare with a garment crossing the chest. A fashion expert might interpret this as the courage of baring one shoulder, and the nobility of keeping one hidden; an idea that would be notable in this era. This is a valid interpretation of the Roman era, nevertheless we are drawing on many centuries to make a single fashion observation, and defining nobility in that epoch is not scalable and does not adequately reflect the broader evolution of consciousness.

Thus, we must move into the political forum to understand the genuine conscious sentiment of the expanding Roman Empire, or, more accurately, universal consciousness of that era. We might say that this epoch was noble, a certain exploration of consciousness in terms of nobility, but first, to only accessing a single vantage point of that aspect. Secondly, it may not be accurate, for we must first understand the state of being in which that notion existed. Although we may now interpret such fashion as noble, for them it may have been seen more as half-naked, like the Greeks, yet civilized like the Romans, especially in dress and decorum.

This understanding only comes when we place ourselves into the Roman mindset, which is, ultimately, an educated guess. From there, we access the sentiment: the dichotomy of decorum versus the exploration of the body as a sexual exemplification. And, of course, the more covert generational discourse between Greeks and Romans regarding pedophilia, something more accepted among the Greeks and scandalous among the Romans, as we have seen in accounts of their emperors.[xii]

Now we have provided a more accurate vantage of that sentiment, but it is one and only of infinite. It relies on the parameters of political discourse and events, because while the political experience is momentary and not definable as a central portal to understanding, it controls the expansion or retraction of consciousness by its activity.

Still, we must understand that battles and political fluctuations are not history in the sense of accessing their form of consciousness, but are merely one of many tools to do so, because of their intersections and their propulsion of future events. One could just as easily grasp Roman consciousness by studying their economy, art, or any other accessible content. The reason we typically do not do so, unless it has lasting relevance in our lives, is because we are only interested in junctures of consciousness that we or parents, grandparents, or great-grandparents experienced. In those cases, we are imprinted with a consciousness sentiment that demands revisiting, for it regulates our psyche.

In the contemporary civilized world, World War II has been imprinted on every psyche, not so much the war itself, but the underlying consciousness to which the war served as a dramatic portal. It is not that the consciousness of the late '30s or early '40s was more significant than that of the late '40s, but that what was expended as consciousness in the late '30s was not entrenched in the political forum until it manifested in the circumstances of the '40s and '50s. The early '30s, too, only gained relevance retroactively, through the lens of what followed. Therefore, to access the consciousness of the '50s without political reference to the war is acutely challenging, since so much of the political process, and thus consciousness, was rooted in it.

The conscious sentiment did not alter from before or after the war, it was simply encapsulated. Once the political regulation receded, the expansion of consciousness resumed. Certain elements were perpetuated by the overexposure to the consciousness of the late '30s, such as the civil rights movement or anti-war sentiment, both tied to World War II but not born within it. The civil rights movement had already been progressing, and anti-war sentiment was strong in the isolationist stance before the war.

Any time we encapsulate consciousness, even when it serves merely as a portal, if it carries attached significance, it may perpetuate itself and trap those engaging with it to the past, even as they believe they are addressing the present. The significance of work culture in the '50s, for example, could be attributed either to an ongoing consciousness sentiment or to the war's encapsulation: the idea that "You see what can be accomplished when you keep your head down." Of course, it could also stem from personal ambition. This is why encapsulating consciousness is so detrimental, it demands allegiance to its evolution and anchors one in the past. In a sense, the encapsulation of consciousness is a form of trauma. These major political moments are complex, precisely because of their vast, ongoing relevance, even as they lead to negative consequences over time.

The Encapsulation of Consciousness in a High-Conscious Environment

Another point that should be mentioned is that the reason we can encapsulate consciousness at such a rate, with so many potent portals, is that we are living in a high-conscious environment. This means that murder, shocking events, and tragedy have become anomalies because we have reached a point where biological deterioration has already been addressed through conscious development, science, policing, oversight, understanding, knowledge, and wisdom. As a result, tragedy, murder, and other dramatic events have become exceptions.

It then falls on the conscious network, or spectrum, to take note of these events when they do occur and to recognize them, not for their biological causality, because, as we have noted, we live in an era with the lowest murder rates and the fewest large-scale wars in comparison to historical precedent. This recognition is not about personal accountability but rather about the process of consciousness itself.

Whether the event is murder, comedic, tragic, or otherwise, it provides us with a nuanced perspective on the circumstances of the time or era. Because we are no longer strictly bound by biological imperatives, and familiarity has been addressed to such an extent, everything becomes representational. The encapsulation and attenuation of concern, therefore, move beyond the realm of personal experience, and consciousness risks becoming wedged. It becomes more about shock and awe, because the sensitivity of one's awareness has become so acute, and the opportunity to encapsulate consciousness arises so frequently.

Chapter Three: The Role of Domestication in Conscious Processing

We often view the lack of domestication in its proper form as the cause of the rampant exposure to the encapsulation of consciousness, preventing the psyche from becoming familiar with its contents. Instead, we can consider this overextension of encapsulation as a process where the psyche processes one encapsulation on top of another, creating a new structure of reality that contests the existing one.

For example, when we become intimate with the subsequent events of a relationship, it's similar to the resurgence of the entire relationship being revealed. At this point, it becomes a new foundation upon which all future relationship exchanges will be based. However, if a new form of intimacy arises without the usual intermediary exchange that makes sense, in other words, without domesticating its contents, the prior intimacy is lost to make room for the new reality. Yet it does not simply vanish; it's pressed into the psyche, which quickly adapts by domestically processing its contents. Technically, it's impossible to experience new consciousness unless one has made room for it. In simpler terms, we cannot interpret a new reality unless we first unveil the current one, and this applies to any form of learning, as explained in another work or as Plato demonstrated.[xiii]

Thus, the sought-after intimacy, again without prior domestication, becomes a momentary, rapid domestication of the previous event. Another, more regular approach is the way a new attempt at intimacy may simply expand upon elements of prior experience. In normal circumstances, this might be the appropriate way forward, such as a wedding day followed by an anniversary, where the anniversary serves as an expansion based on the principles established on the wedding day or its surrounding intimacy. However, more often than not, we tend to expand a newfound intimacy in a way that, rather than simply building on the old form, stretches its elements.

Instead of being a reduced form of intimacy to reflect upon in relation to a loftier one, the prior intimacy is used to sustain any form of intimacy, making the expansion more of a rebellion against the original actualization. While rebellion is often seen as a positive aspect of growth, in this case, it's detrimental to the psyche. The previous content's actualization must now endure an existential fissure, where the current encapsulation no longer properly reflects its source. The original source becomes harder to access, as it now appears outdated in the face of the present moment.

Chapter Four: The Detrimental Effects of Encapsulating Consciousness

Let us begin this discussion with the case of the chosen encapsulation of consciousness, often shaped through social assembly, whether political, artistic, or otherwise, where people collectively identify a center of admiration that becomes an appropriated encapsulation of consciousness. When this occurs repeatedly, one begins to lose access to consciousness in the present moment, or worse, engages with it in a detrimental manner, resulting in a constant tug-of-war between various encapsulations of consciousness, each once believed to be the "true" sentiment of consciousness. Each method is merely a portal to access that sentiment; any could serve the same purpose.

Consciousness is not meant to exist as a static encapsulation, but rather to remain in a continuous flow of exploration, expansion, and retraction; this is the evolution of civilization. Encapsulation is often dictated by social circumstances; and necessarily social, for there is no way to generically encapsulate consciousness beyond the individual level without a collective agreement that represents it as such. Protests in major cities, for example, do not automatically qualify as encapsulations of consciousness unless they align with a relevant social forum and reflect from that process. More so, they do not do so because they do not act upon the experience of current consciousness, but rather as individualized exemplifications of concerning matters. It is only when both the access of current consciousness as it would be, and the social agreement of substantial and diverse participants, are present that it becomes an encapsulation.

Let's take the matter of films, for example. Since there are only a limited number of films released each year, at least those of substantial quality, some are chosen to encapsulate consciousness, presenting such to the audience. This is why the focus on the box office is prevalent, despite the economy post-box office. This is where the film has the opportunity to become an encapsulation of consciousness that is of current value, but only when the themes and sociality intersect in a manner where the puzzle fits in place, so that it can be considered an encapsulation.

However, this is chosen by the sociality of the participants, whether conceptually or physically, which then results in the loss, the detrimental loss, of the current consciousness flow. For now, consciousness is lost because it has been abridged or abbreviated in the encapsulation, which, in other forms, would only process itself during wartime. But now, it is chosen for the possibly altruistic benefit of taking a sample of consciousness. This is detrimental because it limits the scope and criteria of consciousness, with anything going forward being bound within that encapsulation.

There is a type of consciousness that is subliminal which continues despite encapsulation, unless that encapsulation is all-encompassing across every part of the hierarchy, whether political or otherwise. But in general, there will not be an encapsulation of the entirety of that consciousness flow. Yet, individually, one can encapsulate consciousness through certain methods, particularly if, for instance, they lack a context for approaching, for instance, a film and instead choose to use the film as a means to intersect with the sentiment of consciousness. In doing so, they are bound to that consciousness experience, so that anything follows that sentiment.

This is a healthy process if the encapsulation serves as a method of breaking the domestication of consciousness, bringing home the consciousness experience without the need to constantly remain in attenuation to the flow of consciousness. But it becomes detrimental when it is used to assume that this is the foremost reality. Since it is a conscious experience it can be mistaken for reality itself, such that anything frontward is not that, and anything behind is external of that.

One might then believe that this is not a portal to consciousness, but rather consciousness itself.

This is why we have the concept of political violence, whether external or domestic, as a form of injecting small measures of violence into a vast population. In such a population, violence of this magnitude occurs daily in various forms, but in this context, such acts of violence become centered due to the fact that the populace is in constant attenuation to newly formatted encapsulations of consciousness. This makes it remarkably easy to jar the political spectrum and public thought; even low-level acts, drastic or controversial, can reach into the private sphere of a household. This occurs precisely because of the constant desire for direct encounters with encapsulated consciousness. Political violence only functions within a specific societal structure because the constant pursuit of attenuation to encapsulations of consciousness keeps all eyes fixed forward, searching for any element, whether it intersects with current reality, a preliminary memory, or a substandard form.

Certain manifestations of political violence may be remnants of an earlier form of consciousness, yet they are perceived as presently relevant simply because they occur today. If we were to look back at historical societies, we would see that individuals once deliberately avoided attenuating to encapsulations of consciousness, recognizing the detrimental effects and psychological complications that such encapsulation entails.

We often assume that tragedy or centered attenuation is a one-way street, but that is not entirely accurate. A complete attenuation to the political spectrum, whether to its representatives or to the government as a whole, can intersect with consciousness to such an extent that it is presumed to be reality itself.

For example, in the case of a political manifestation perceived as detrimental, it is not that encapsulation is necessary to experience consciousness, but rather that encapsulation itself is mistaken for reality.

Consequently, whatever the political element may be, no alternative sequence is seen as viable. A perceived notion of criminality or complication may thus be interpreted as tragic, whether it affects one's individuality or that of an empathetic other. In this way, political ramifications arise whereby encapsulation extends beyond the personal and comes to be presumed as the entirety of reality. The political entity is then pursued for dominating or regulating one's life or the world at large.

There is a reason why the act of warfare is separated from the general populace. We do not want the hands of violence to belong to the infrastructure itself. Rather, violence must be compartmentalized, so that the system is not seen as a murderous regime, but as a process: an inevitability of protection and governance. Just as the General is not the President, the President is not the General. They must remain separate to maintain this compartmentalization, not as a critique, but because no individual can be presumed to carry the full weight of the process, from the intention behind a tragedy to its ultimate result. It is important to recognize that the political entity is not a single person holding that responsibility, but rather a complex arena of dynamics. Even if one were to follow the General further, it would not be the General alone, and likewise, it is not the President alone but correspondingly there is advisors, committees, and so on, such that the activity of the political entity, and its tragic processes, are distributed across thousands, if not millions, of people.

But this very framing reflects the perspective of someone who encapsulates a political sentiment, especially in relation to its tragic aspect, such that they do not treat it as the full intersection of consciousness, but rather as an episodic element contained by it. For what is the interest in the political intersection, if not to gain access to consciousness itself? That access is not about the tragic element alone, but about the intersection in conjunction with it.

It is this encapsulation of the political entity as a realm of consciousness that causes an individual to become fixed to one side of the experience. They may come to believe either that the political realm embodies a malicious tragic arm, or that it stands in total opposition to consciousness, even though it is often through the political realm that access to consciousness arises. Alternatively, they may perceive the government, not as a political entity, but as a system of processes; an encapsulation of consciousness from which there is no escape; it becomes tyrannical. Either way, the individual becomes fixed within that encapsulation, assuming it to be reality itself, when, in fact, it is merely one of many potent portals to access consciousness.

In this case empathy follows a fixated political portal intersecting with consciousness. Once fixated, it is assumed that reality is nothing but this tragic arm, or worse, that the perfection of tragedy avoidance, unlike statesmanship (which is impossible in such a realm), becomes one's very existence. They are then in opposition to their own existence, having chosen this portal and no other.

On the other hand, empathy comes first: the individual is empathetic to themselves, yet recognizes the overreach of government in their daily life. They are thus compelled to encapsulate such consciousness against their will, usually when no other form of consciousness is available. This often occurs when their structural environment is so far removed from real civilization. In such a case, they become oppositional to the same government entity.

More importantly, when someone understands domestication, that they must become familiar with that which they encapsulate, they do so properly and consistently; as a result they no longer seek further encapsulations. They become engaged with their current domesticity. Later, when it is time to seek attenuation again, they prefer something private, something individual, not generic, and certainly not the product of radical acts, tragedies, or shock-awe that demand attention. While shock-awe does intersect with consciousness, it often results in an overdose of it, depriving one of the preliminary and private development necessary for true awareness.

If someone is structurally confined, perhaps living in suburbia or another form of isolated locality, they may adjust their conscious attenuation in problematic ways. Either the process of actualizing their domesticity becomes a troubling outcome, or, assuming that they have earned the right of passage and reach the central realm where all consciousness flows to and from, they encounter shock-awe via direct informational material linked to conscious sentiment. This offers everything except a true conscious experience. It is not real, but experienced as pseudo-real, so they receive the existential risk without the genuine experience, and lose their domestication in the process as this is perceived as an external access.

Of course, we do not selectively choose the encapsulations of consciousness. If one is not directly affected by a traumatic event, then in that moment they are compelled into an encapsulation and must follow it coherently. For the rest of society, however, empathy becomes a trick of the psyche; for they are neither aligned with nor familiar with that substrate of experience. Yet they step into it to encapsulate consciousness, which is the real aim. Were their concern genuinely empathetic, they would be attuned to the constant, normalized violence of the world; or to the ever-present strategic motions that rarely become political. In other words, they would recognize that not all intersections with consciousness are tragic.

We may dispute the effects of these episodes, but they are called tragedies for a reason. Tragedy is the narrative arc that teaches, granting catharsis over emotions. More often, however, these encapsulations or tragic forms are employed as mechanisms to direct attention toward consciousness, delivered at a steady rate, keeping one perpetually fixed to current consciousness, resistant to domestication, estranged from the private flow of experience, and, above all, bound to the specific and generic portals through which consciousness is accessed.

For example, in a population of seven or eight billion, there will be tragedies, major ones, which, in some ways, can be considered encapsulations of consciousness due to their drastic effects and resonance with consciousness itself. However, when this is done through generic forms, it fails to account for the quality of consciousness, which would not be continuously defined or encapsulated to perform well by the constant normality of tragedy.

This is not limited to tragedy. Any form of encapsulation, even the renowned individual, positions itself as an intersection of consciousness. Yet, a private trait that is exceptionally superior does not necessarily translate to consciousness. If there is a gathering of momentum, it may be that the populace is following a memory of consciousness, one that no longer receives present reception, or may be forming a suboptimal level, which is never ideal. Socially, the momentum merely proves that it is based on a form of consciousness, not that it intersects with the present movement of consciousness.

Sociality can emerge in any system, but if there is a lack of diversity, it proves that the moment is not intersecting with current consciousness, since it follows a specific contextual direction rather than reflecting through varied forms of personhood, each of which finds its own entrance. This proves that participants are concerned with the portal rather than the consciousness from which it leads.

If we asked such representatives whether they are intersecting with consciousness, they would likely admit they are merely expressing a specific talent or quality, not the true home of consciousness, but fulfilled to intersect in a moment of momentum.

Additionally, certain encapsulations may not be true at all. They do not serve current consciousness but instead produce shock and awe that appears godlike, or like an act of consciousness, when in fact they are merely expressions of nature or lower forms of consciousness, lacking real value. One might argue that there is some divine expression in a tragedy in a marginal country, but its resonance is so faint compared to the current momentum of consciousness that the encapsulation becomes distorted. One does not travel to such a place to encounter consciousness; they may go for research or sabbatical. Thus, such consciousness exists only at a diminished degree. Instead, one should remain on the sidelines and seek either a private encapsulation in a space of comfort, or a proper intersection with political mobility or other form that embodies a higher encapsulation, one that does not diminish their development.

To treat encapsulation as the proper approach to reality is, in fact, its negation. When one departs from an encapsulation, they remain bound to its sentiment and must domesticate such before moving forward. If they attempt to enter another without doing so, the psyche begins to defragment. They become confined within a domesticated framework, unable to take on a new one, left without a clear sense of their own intonation.

Sometimes this occurs without our input or control. But if the process is repeated, and a constant stream of attempted encapsulations is present, the psyche fragments. One loses a stable seat from which to endure personhood. There is no consistency between experiences of consciousness or the psyche's structure of reality. The pressing issue arising from a constant attenuation to encapsulation is that once a specific content is perceived, not merely as one approach to the general flow, but as somehow specialized or significant in its own right, it leads to that content being seen as the only structure of reality, and even more so, that no other reality exists. Instead of being an interaction where one chooses to participate in the flow through these bridges of content, it becomes an almost involuntary experience, where the informative aspect is not an internal dialogue but already formatted to be received, or recognized at its latest stage of development.

In the usual case, one focuses on their personal perspective of general consciousness, which may serve as a portal for that process. However, instead, it is perceived without one's contextual separation, with such material directly linked to an encapsulation of consciousness. Thus, consciousness enters in its raw form and is viewed as true in its specificity, despite being only one of an infinite number of approaches to the general flow.

PART VI: FROM POLITICAL THEORY TO PRACTICE; SYMBOLS, STORIES & SYSTEMIC RESPONSE

Chapter One: The Symbolic Hierarchy of Aesthetic Prowess and Class Structure

Does this emerging symbolic hierarchy of aesthetic prowess constitute a formalized divergent class structure, or is it merely an illusory construct rooted in the experience of a particular subgroup? Moreover, will it extend to encompass a broader political significance, or will it remain confined to reciprocal interactions solely within that subgroup, thereby distinguishing itself from conventional modes of social exchange?

The entire notion of performative behavior is that it is a performance upon a setting for which the genuine framework of interpretation is considered the only metric of political substantiation. To perform is to embody a sentiment from which it ascends from that general framework, and in itself does little to hold a role within the social spectrum. A performer is one who understands the audience more than any other trail, including all the content for which the performance is embedded, e.g., writer.

The audience can be extrapolated in various ways, succeeding in any regard, one which does not illuminate how the audience leans toward the adaptability of the performer in vitalizing the audience. We understand little of the audience from the interest of the performer, nor do we understand the performer in its content, as its characteristic is extrapolating for the receptivity of the audience. In this way, we cannot divulge an informational theme from either vantage, as they are both embedded in the performance-audience relationship that supersedes the specific performance and its ramifications. It is this very notion which has the audience fairly limited in influence over a performance based on its innate content, for if that were the case,

Hamlet should have sealed the door in the disillusionment of pinnacle irony, existential residence, and revenge, all of which had not fulfilled the theme but rather may have exacerbated it. The performance does not enter into communion with the specific content because it is more noted for that relationship, and especially the emotive layer that is allowed the freedom of expression by both audience and performer.[xiv]

It would not necessarily be the case that such a development defines a class structure, for class is usually embedded within the broader framework of a social system rather than something generational. To assert class based on generational attributes is to diverge from familial structures, appearing instead as a self-contained rerun of their usual dynamic function. A performance does so because of a very specific relationship with the audience, for which in the ever-evolving sociality, that audience may change from minute to minute, thus disgracing the entire performance, let alone attributing it as a part of the class system.

In respect to the digital era, it would seem that this phenomenon is being regarded as a certain form of class structure, insofar as normal dialogue or cultural transmission is no longer central. Rather, these individuals are treated primarily as consumers, with marketing as the ultimate objective. It is almost as though the generation in question are avatars of an internet phase, rather than real people. It is difficult to attribute the emergence of this dynamic solely to the influence of the internet. A more plausible explanation is that it is grounded in a wider generational theme.

Chapter Two: The Illusion of Biological Continuity in Global Political Constructs

This political entity, which we can term the "globalized entity," profits from the term *humanity* as an axiomatic notion, thereby allowing itself to proliferate as the arbitrator of biological continuance and other "human"-related endeavors, e.g., globalist altruism. However, this is only a fragment of the political concept itself and never supersedes its political construct. Any bridging of social systems or beings becomes part of a particular political formation and must act according to its parameters. Therefore, what is constituted as biological continuity is simply the mannerisms of its internal constitution, making no claim upon scientific reality.[xv]

For instance, one can view a single organism, especially a single higher life form, as having the potential and ability to proliferate itself more so than the majority of humanity. From this viewpoint, based on their level of health, conceptual development, and other elements that allow for singular continuity to outweigh humanity, they would not be considered under such a political entity, which is specifically concerned with the collection of all humanity. A single individual who may proliferate for a trillion years to come may be argued by the *globalized political entity* as something that cannot be controlled and, therefore, although pressing as an issue and possibility, must be denigrated to continue the political construct.

Notice how the same argument applies to any group or state when something is beyond its constitution, such as another state or broader group. They argue that they can only control based on their perspective, and if they allow a broader perspective or possibility, it would not be able to assist their internal process. The argument does not emanate from a true manifestation of the internal form's nature but rather functions as a byproduct to avoid viewing the construct beyond its parameters. Understandably, the state does not want to view itself beyond its parameters. The group does not want to see beyond itself, consequently it justifies the very notion of existent groups by asserting that attending to a broader group would cause a loss of the intricacy and nuance of its internal perspective.

If, for instance, we were to say that it would be better for humanity in the next trillion years if all its organisms, especially higher life forms, were decimated, allowing a reversion to earlier cellular formations to reconstitute themselves, much like a caterpillar's metamorphosis to a butterfly, this globalized political entity would not account for or consider such a process. They are not concerned with the true nature of biological continuity but rather with the political entity and its construct, in which *humanity* is simply another term for *citizen*, and *political continuity* is another term for the proliferation of its continuance as a political construct.

The state inherently does not care for the citizen; it attends to the proliferation of the construct called the state and will sacrifice every single citizen to continue that process. In our case, the globalized political entity focuses on biological continuity as a way to assert citizenship and statesmanship for every individual under its rubric which happens to include all higher life forms.

If they argue that the metamorphosis is too long-term and therefore continuity must be based on relative short-term terms, we ask: for what reason do they set the parameters so short when they claim to care about biological continuity? They may answer that it is because they cannot control biological continuity at that scale, to which we simply observe a string of justifications designed to retain parameters that allow the political construct to continue as is.

To strengthen this point, we demonstrate that such reasoning is simply an aggrandized version of the political entity's logic. If we follow what is termed *humanity*, it requires the same sacrifice of some humanity for the proliferation of the whole; just like the state sacrifices some individuals to continue its political construct. The question then becomes: to what extent, and to whom, is the expense worth it?

For the state, it is simpler, they consider everyone worthwhile, but the representations of the state, or the more civilized elements, to be more significant, as that is where the epicenter lies. Similarly, the globalized political entity will expend every higher life form for its proliferation but views the sacrificial elements as those least attributed to its epicenters or representative stature. This is worrisome, as it differs from the regular state, which at least contests opposing systems through warfare and disputes. Here, the globalized entity's constitution demands that to maintain its role, it must renounce every strand of higher life form.

The state as an institution weakens as it expends more citizenship; its capacity for expenditure declines so that it does not self-annihilate, similar to how institutions wither by selective failure at the individual level, weakening adherence to its model, one without personification. However, this leads to a deadlock: although the state's epicenter is the most civilized aspect of the state, the globalized political entity cannot assert itself as the most civilized aspect of its internal state. It does not concern itself with the continuity of civilization, but rather with the continuity of biological form.

If they argue that continuity of biological form equals continuity of civilized elements, they must choose between the two. If they prioritize the continuance of civilization over humanity, they must sacrifice humanity to civilization. If they prioritize biological form, they must sacrifice civilization for biology. Evolutionarily speaking, biological continuity is likely not bound to civilized elements but rather to internal biological processes.

If they choose to define the globalized political entity as a constitution of biological continuity, their entire process must focus accordingly. The epicenter, or least sacrificial claim, would then be where stronger biological continuance can be ensured, leading to differentiation between those biologically adept for continuance and those who are not, a notion they are clearly unprepared to entertain.

Alternatively, if they base their constitution on the continuance of civilization, they will not primarily concern themselves with humanity or biological continuity, but with civilization; an entity inseparable from biology but not fundamentally required by biological systems themselves. Civilization rests on biological systems but is sustained by its own contractual and theoretical frameworks.

Thus, the outcome of a strictly politicized globalized system would either focus on preserving certain biological features at the expense of others; which seems improbable as a scientific endeavor given its complexity, like arbitrating evolution with trillions of variables influenced by unpredictable environmental hazards, or sacrifice all humanity to preserve civilization. We must then ask: what reason is there for a politicized constitution created by humanity if it disregards the biological systems that underpin the very minds adhering to that framework?

Moving beyond critical analysis, it is probable for a globalized political entity to exist as long as it views itself as any other state; its constitution based on a larger membership base but acting with the same procedures. The critique arises only when it extends beyond that spectrum, making analysis difficult due to a proliferation that may be detrimental both to its members and to the understanding of those involved in its expansion.

If, for example, it embraces continuity of civilization, much like how academia preserves the tradition of civilization, it can formulate itself without involving all humanity, just as academia does not include everyone. It would thus appear to stand for the continuity of civilization rather than any specific state. In this case, the least sacrificial elements would be those fitting a less civilized criterion, while the higher and least sacrificial elements would be those closest to civilized elements. However, this logic leads to a conundrum because of its radical implications for people as a whole, likely causing reluctance to proceed.

If, instead, the constitution is formulated as biological continuity, then it remains a political constitution, not a true continuation of biological continuity, based on previous arguments. Once this is accepted, it becomes an arbitrary arrangement of biological continuity. However, this too is pressured, as one must defend biological continuity by making sacrifices of elements that impede the process, while adhering to those that promote it. If the least civilized groups turn out to be most biologically adept, civilization itself must be sacrificed.

Moreover, this invites the complicated conundrum of misappropriating what constitutes biological continuity, distinguishing higher from lower life forms, and determining scientific feasibility, all of which, even if resolved, carry the risk of imprudence. Choosing one direction might overlook a key factor that could undermine the entire process and act contrary to the constitution it aims to protect.

The political entity which we view as a globalized entity, profits from the term *humanity* as an axiomatic notion, thereby allowing itself to proliferate as the arbitrator of biological continuance and other 'human' related endeavors, e.g., globalist altruism. However, this is a fragment of the political concept itself and never supersedes its political construct. Any bridging of social systems or beings would become a part of a certain political formation and should act according to its parameters. Therefore, what is constituted as biological continuity is simply the mannerisms of its internal constitution, yet makes no claim upon scientific reality.[xvi]

For instance, one can view a single organism, especially a single higher life form, as having the potential and ability to proliferate itself more so than the majority of humanity, and in this viewpoint, based on their level of health, conceptual development, and all those elements which allow singular continuity to outweigh humanity, will not be considered under such a political entity; for they are specifically concerned about the collection of all of humanity. A single individual who may proliferate for a billion years may be argued by the *globalized political entity* as something that cannot be controlled for, and thereby, although seems pressing as an issue and possibility, must be denigrated in order to continue the political construct.

Notice how that same argument would be considered for any group or state when it is mentioned that there is something beyond its constitution, such as another state or broader group, where they simply argue that they could only control based on their perspective, so that if they allow the broader perspective or possibility, they would not be able to assist in their internal process. The argument is not emanating from a true manifestation of the nature of that internal form, but rather as a byproduct to avoid viewing the construct from beyond its parameters. The state simply does not want to view itself beyond its state's parameters, understandably so. The group does not want to view beyond itself, thereby it must justify the very notion of existent groups by asserting that if they were to attend to the broader group, they would lose the intricacy and nuance of their internal perspective.

If, for instance, we were to say that it is for the betterment and longevity of humanity for the next billion years if all its organisms, especially higher life forms, were decimated, such that a reversion to earlier formations of cellular structure can reconstitute itself, much like a metamorphosis of a caterpillar to a butterfly, this would be a case where the globalized political entity cannot account or consider; they would oppose such a dictation. They are not concerned with the true nature of biological continuity, but rather with the political entity and its construct, to which *humanity* is simply another term for *citizen*, and *political continuity* is another term for the proliferation of its continuance as a political construct.

The general state does not inherently care for the citizen; they attend to the proliferation of the construct that is considered the state, and they will sacrifice every single citizen in order to continue that process. But in our case, the globalized political entity is focusing on biological continuity as a way to assert citizenship and statesmanship for every individual that falls under their rubric, which so happens to include all higher life forms.

We will cement this point, although any logical following of this process would notice it is exactly the same as the political entity, just simply an aggrandized version of that. If we follow what is termed *humanity*, such will require that same sacrifice of some humanity for the proliferation of the whole of humanity; just like the state would sacrifice some in order for the continuance of its political construct. The question then becomes: for how much, and to whom, is it worth the expense?

For the state, it is simpler, for they would consider everybody worthwhile, and only the representations of the state to be more significant, or the more civilized elements of the state, for that is where the epicenter lies. Yet we find this might be the same for the globalized political entity, where they will expense every single higher life form for the proliferation of that political entity, yet will view the sacrificial elements as those least attributed to its epicenters and its representational elements. Worrisome as differentiating from the regular state, which at least has warfare to dispel contesting systems, in this case, it is its constitution to maintain its role that it must sacrifice every strand of higher life form. The state as an institution will weaken as it expenses more of citizenship base, where its ability of expenditure grows weaker so that it does not self-annihilate. Similar to how institutions wither, by selective failure at the individual level, which then weakens the adherence to its model. In this case it leads them to a deadlock, because although the state's epicenter is that of the most civilized process of the state, this globalized political entity cannot be asserted as the most civilized process of its internal state, for they are not concerning themselves with continuity of civilization, but rather continuity of biological form.

It is as if we offer the lever of biological continuity to the globalized entity, only for them to make decisions without the knowledge or fortitude to understand what true biological continuity entails, thereby creating a course that runs opposite to their intended way.

Chapter Three: Secondary Narratives and the Conflict of Resolution

A narrative never presupposes a conflict, although in retrospect it appears as though a narrative created the present conflict. Rather, it is only the formation of a secondary narrative, one which views the conflict of the primary narrative through the lens of a novel narrative arc. The secondary narrative is such that it claims an inborn conflict laden in the prior narrative is, in fact, an emanation of a different narrative. However, with a simple logical inference, one notes that this secondary narrative has an embedded conflict, of which it is the causation. The objective of a secondary narrative is to postulate that all conflict is based on a narrative, rather than presupposing it. In some sense, it is the attempt at providing the ultimate narrative function, one which diverges every aspect of the conflict such that it would no longer be called a conflict.

A narrative is individualistic to each proposition of said narrative, and to another, it would be a newfound narrative. Even sharing the same story, most common of all being *original sin*, each participant experiences an individualistic narrative arc. Although the objective conflict is according to the analysis of that story, the participant and observer of the narrative contain their relatable conflict, to which they find resolution based on that premise. The point is that, because narratives are individualistic, they find resolution on a personal level. When a team wins, the individualistic conflict now finds resolution based on the objective outcome of the victory. This explains the manifestation of degeneration in a city following a victory: although it would seem a resolution for the objective narrative, at each individual arc, the conflict seems to be finding a differing resolution than that of the objective victory.

The reason why Sara Cobb (2013) of George Mason University noted the need for complex narratives in lieu of simpler ones, such as diversity training, is that such training dutifully attempts to avoid the present conflict that would eventually lead to the formation of a narrative structure. Take, for instance, diversity training: if we were to confer a narrative arc to any conflict as the empathic reconstitution of diversity upon the other side, we approach a different problem. The newfound narrative structure has not engaged the specific material of the conflict, such that the metaphysical role of diversity is not followed thoroughly to the specific conflict it attempts to solve.

This only compounds another narrative, compelling a new formation of the inbred conflict that is found in every narrative. Not only has the narrative function failed to correspond to the opposing sides of a conflict, it has allowed the dissemination of a new conflict that is intrinsic to every narrative structure. In other words, we can find narrative functions that do provide haven from the original conflict, yet do the aforementioned work of secondary narrative-building. Instead of reconciling the conflicting ends through a metaphysical correlation, the secondary narrative entices the notion that the emanation of the conflict itself is none other than a narrative within itself. More troubling than the former, it expounds the conflict twofold, seeking the details of the secondary narrative to prove in what way the primary conflict is really not considered a conflict at all. Secondary narratives ground the very premise of the conflict to the nth degree, without any retribution to its logic, which will be found to form a cyclical pattern: avoiding conflict in order to postulate that all that is contained is but a narrative arc.

Cobb continues, "Particularly in the context of conflict, idealized speech situations are not available to marginalized speakers" (Cobb, 2013, p. 10), which essentially allows for a secondary narrative function, one that notes the inability of a subject to make known the very conflict they are attempting to resolve. Although there is coherence in the premise of this secondary narrative (that subjects are not equally represented in a conflict), this only serves to continue the first conflict that all are attempting to resolve. In this way, the first (and only) conflict requires a resolution of the secondary narrative, which will not be found other than by disallowing the premise of searching for a secondary narrative. If we attempt, rather presumptuously, to provide a correlating factor to resolve the secondary factor, it would look like this:

Conflict – subjects are not equal in the conflict;

Correlating Factor – nature cannot serve equals in every situation;

Resolution – marginalized conflict is not a singular importance in approaching conflict.

This is the only method for dealing with a secondary narrative, for the purpose, as all would agree, for the initial conflict. If the attempt is made to provide for the marginalized factor, then we are proclaiming elements that partake in the conflict in order to fix the problem, which coincidentally highlights the disparity of the conflict. Enlarging the elements of the conflict will always enlarge the conflict itself, until a resolution is found for the secondary narrative, or the ideation of supporting narratives that do not serve the conflict is dismissed.

—"Narrative strands are, by definition, not idiosyncratic to an individual, they are held in and by a group. However, the geography of narrative within an identity group is not uniform, every strand will contain substrands; these substrands share a narrative DNA with the main strand and together they comprise the narrative landscape as a system of narratives" (Bernardi, 2012).

Bernardi (2012) is thus applying physical systems to metaphysical inquiry. As we have noted, narrative structures are always somewhat metaphysical, for they correlate to physical factors, in the case of human conflict, two individualistic makeups. They do not inherently adjoin, and only through a narrative function do we find the connection between individuals who are materially distinct entities. So in defining "narrative strands," surely there is a network chain to every metaphysical application, but there is an impossibility of resolution if we view the correlating factor as part of an intrinsic network.[xvii]

That would only accentuate the initial conflict tenfold, to the point where it appears that resolution is not the purpose but rather being the host of a continued and submissive narrative chain. Surely the premise is true, as all metaphysical notions do participate in an ecosystem that far exceeds any one aspect, but each of these parts on the chain is in fact host to another conflict. Not only do we fail to provide resolution to the current conflict with a complex narrative, as noted by Cobb, but we also add a secondary narrative compounded on each other, each containing its own innate conflict, and each requiring a unique narrative function for its genuine resolution.

"According to Schechtman's 'narrative self-constitution view', a view with which I am in basic agreement, the construction of an identity-constituting autobiographical narrative does not have to be self-conscious." (Nelson, 2001)[xviii]

This is a very charged premise, which explains the construction of a narrative structure, in that it does not follow the personal nature of the individual or the broader narrative associations. For the very reason that narratives are, in fact, correspondences of conflict, whatever situation of conflict exists, it is there that the narrative is found. One can participate in an identity, such that now they are part of the conflict and thus the narrative, or depart from that intimacy, to which they are now far away from the conflict. Even personal conflict enacts the same premise, where one who finds themselves in separation from another is experiencing the true nature of individuality. It is rather the opposite in personal situations, where the narrative function is what allows connection to continue, and all can attest to a breakdown in narrative function with family bodies which soon serve its degeneration.

We would not go so far as to spell out the agency of a narrative function as Nelson (2001) has furthered: "Counter stories, then, are tools designed to repair the damage inflicted on identities by abusive power systems. They are purposive acts of moral definition, developed on one's own behalf or on behalf of others."

Surely, as mentioned, one can supplement a value or justification to a conflict and only later apply a narrative function, not so much to correlate the conflicting sides, but to apply a new value to the lot. Yet still, the value is not what the systems are after; rather, correlating the conflict is their objective. And the utilization of the narrative function is the correct order of progress: conflict, narrative, justification, and resolution.

Counter stories are not facets of preemptive measures of insurance or control, but merely the process of enduring a conflict which threatens to continue with disparity and degenerate the whole system to which both sides of the conflict are embedded. When a conflict endures without the necessary counter story, it is not to the detriment of the identity, group, or individual alone, but to the entire premise to which both sides of the conflict are affected. Not only is the political representative, for instance, enduring a breakdown in their representative stature, but also the populace is further entrenched in the inability of being represented upon.

Counter stories are not mechanisms of control but rather the natural process to endure the system that lies behind the conflict. Thus, counter stories, or the continuing process of the narrative function, is not only important for the conflict at hand but for the system to which the conflict rests upon.

Chapter Four: The Constructs of Existential Risk: Individual, Institutional, and Conceptual Domains

When we invoke the view of existential risk, we must first formulate: in the criteria of existence, what are we discussing? Despite the notion of something being considered existential as furthering the discussion of its constitution, for that it is existential and more elementary to whatever comes after it, we utilize the term as a manner of circumventing the very process and chain of logicality. One could thus say that a lack of procreation is an existential risk, for the existence of the eugenics will be halted, and biological organization will follow a degenerative factor. Yet, we could also dictate that if we were to view all of humanity, or a subgroup under the prerogative of concern, then a halt to a single individual with their respective procreation is not an existential threat. More so, if all of humanity were to cease to procreate, while a single individual makes the choice to procreate, it would still not invoke the notion of being an existential risk. Rather, the arena of concern is the first formation of the succeeding proclamation of existential risk, and with this in mind we must turn to the very construct that allows for a specific area of concern.

We can thus differentiate the categories of concern: humanity, civilization, subgroups such as identities or states, familial groups, and finally, the individual. There can be an existential risk to humanity yet not for civilization, such as a downloaded system that retains the theoretical framework of civilization; for civilization but not for humanity, such as marginalized populations; as well for an individual in contrast to any of the other groupings. Besides these, there is the existential risk of any construct, like that of an idea, such as democracy, or a relationship, such as the existential risk of a relationship regarding infidelity. Therefore, whenever we decide to utilize the term for an inquiry, more so we are invoking the construct or criteria to which we are pledging allegiance to a point where we can consider it existentially important. For the individual, their lifespan can be considered more significant than all of humanity, thereby its complete degradation would not be constituted as an existential risk. In fact, if the inquiry is made on an individual level, it would be impractical to concern oneself with broader existential risks. For why would the individual find democracy, or subgroups, or all of civilization an important topic to the point of claiming existential territory, if they are separated from that by being an existent entity of its own weight? The only way it would seem practical to even view humanity in a cluster, or civilization, or even subgroups, is when the concern is not individualist or personal, but institutional. The state can concern itself with its innate existential bearing and thus provision such as an existential risk with the manifestation of military strength. Humanity, when invoked as such, would be a globalized institution that might be called the general constitution of a state, whereby in that department it can concern itself with humanity's existential risk. Without this globalized institution, there is no reason to cluster all of humanity under that same group and even more to consider it as being an existential entity. It is possible that there are threatening things that can decimate humanity, much like there are for any particular individual, by both being mortal entities. But the fact that humanity may seem to broach more risk does not mean we follow its system as an entity, that is, unless we arrive from the institutional perspective of a globalized political entity, which thus represents humanity but is more about its members than the higher life form aspect. Just as a state may view its citizens as part of its existential factor, sacrificing some for the betterment of its existence, they are not viewed by their virtue of being a higher life form or biological significance, but more so because they are members of that group. When we invoke the political entity which seems to carry globalized members, it is merely the abridgment of a higher amount of population, rather than anything more than another construct.

We can use terms like humanity, or higher life form, or biological continuity to add glare to this political entity; just as a state may view their citizens as part of the economic engine, even as they are not built as economic entities. The term humanity is rather arbitrary, but merely allows a political entity to take allowance and determination for more populace, and can be seen as an attempt of power and control. For once the term humanity is invoked, this political globalized entity can now include more manpower and can be seen as expansive to a point where critique of its very political underpinnings seems not to appear, and thus are demarcated for all people under the namesake of *humanity* to concern with this existential risk as if it were that significant.

Chapter Five: Real-Time Evolution and Collective Cognition

With this distinction in mind, we now turn to a detailed examination of how a globalized political entity frames biological continuity as an existential necessity; thus blurring the line between institutional survival and actual existential risk.

Evolutionary lineage presents a query among the embodied members of its subclass, so that we can identify a process of thinking that pertains only to that lineage. Different from most studies, the two sides of the spectrum are transparently laid out before we begin the research. On one side, we have the traditional demand to maintain and retain whatever has been evolutionarily imprinted upon the organism. The second side is the juncture of real-time movement onto which many different modes of interaction cause the organism to redirect its path and begin the arduous process of imprinting a new adaptation that may not coincide with all prior lineage and its generational work. The very nature of this has the conflicting effect of appearing that inquiry and its process have already been explored.

Contrary to that supposition, in the knowledge of the various processes which occur, we can understand which choices may result as being supplementary for a more holistic higher life form structure and what will be counterintuitive to adapt in the final stage. However, even with an entire inquiry, we would not be able to envision the outcome for the various elements that can never be foreseen. Yet, we would still become aware that it will be presumed to be unsatisfactory unless many changes occur before its outcome.

For instance, an attempted adaptation for males to give birth may result in a satisfactory outcome for the individual and society. Indeed, henceforth, we would need to know the entire civilized structure and its familial basis which will be usurped without a presiding version to take its place; presumably, that society and the individual will not progress when perceived in this entirety. Second to every evolutionary notion is the reason for its pursuit, requiring a weighty theory and philosophical basis for the implementation of such drastic adaptations. Surely we can perceive how this study is useful when we prepare to gain more access to evolutionary adaptations without its required waiting period.

The waiting period is a process in normal evolutionary terms and will be in accordance with biological survival. However, this is a misconception, for it can only process the future in reference to a preliminary system of understanding. The system does not know that, for instance, anger is the cause of much biological demise, yet it is there to protect biological life. We could assume that if we were conceptually aware of this fact for many generations, anger would have adapted to presume the complexity of biological threats and would not be a detrimental cause.

We can see that the waiting period of evolutionary adaptation is not in service to biological life but is a reality of the evolutionary process. Immediate adaptation on an evolutionary timescale is reserved for transparent biological threats that can be surmised more easily by the evolutionary adaptation process. To prevent a complex biological threat, one will not find assistance in the adaptation process but in another likely locale, that of the conceptual domain.

We can even conjure that the conceptual domain has been an adaptation because of the noticed buffer of the normal adaptation process. Instead, a real-time computing device can follow immediate changes with the caveat of being unable to change the biological framework from within. To understand why this device has not been given that access is due to the element of power. A major biological change may be induced only to deal with unforeseen circumstances according to the complex dynamics of nature. A single failure of a single organism can have drastic repercussions upon all organic life, which is a power that the evolutionary system is not willing to partake. Even as the promise is also an unforeseen future with such abilities, understandably the normal waiting period of the organic structure was deemed proper to slowly adapt without disrupting the system of dynamics.

However, it can also be foreseen that the cognitive process will eventually become so potent in understanding reality that it will gain access despite the evolutionary choice. This must have been seen as inevitable, and we must understand the objective having initiated the cognitive process. The solution was that the cognitive process would be tied to all other cognitive engines, so that its only process of growth would require the attention of the entire system of higher life forms. This would incorporate the element of the complex dynamics that may be harmed by a singular proposal, and this communal activation would require a unanimous vote upon singular evolutionary choices. Even as the individual may be able to activate the evolutionary choice from the privacy of their unique domain, to gain access to that level of information would have them embedded into the communal sphere, thus being an expression of communal affairs even as they remain in the private domain. A single cognitive process will not be able to access evolutionary choice because it requires not only a database of knowledge but also of communal diversity.

This is why we have a certain veneration for individuals who produce harm in the social realm through mental and physical devices that are produced through communal complexity. When there is a highly complex cognitive process that produces harm, there is a fascination for it being an expression of the entire communal engine. Having displayed their rearing contained by that system, it makes us wonder how the very cognitive system that we all ascribe is finding a seemingly harmful expression.

Only to conclude one of two things: the communal cognitive engine is in decline and these are examples of its demise, as individuals who have gained from its realm only to be unable to match in sociality and fail in the privacy of their affairs; or the more fearsome notion that they have only produced what the cognitive engine had expressed in clear terms, that it seeks to self-destruct; that we attach to a system that seeks our demise.

Some material developments will compel the communal sphere to attach all its resources and complexity in order to gain access to their full potency. For instance, nuclear power will always be something embedded in the social hierarchy even if all its knowledge is known and all materials available. The communal enterprise will ensure that its power distributed among the entire system so that if an individual makes a choice, it can be concluded that it emanates from the entire communal system.

Every part of the chain that gives access to that power will be well-ordered by the entirety of the communal body, and one who understands its complexity will be required to be reared and educated within those communal centers. By having the knowledge, it would be abundantly clear that they are part of a philosophical lineage that would never lead to the demise of higher life forms. Of course, it is upon everybody to gain systematic knowledge of nuclear power, but to have the embodied complexity that would offer full freedom to such power will only be available to those who follow a direct educational tradition.

We must remember that any scientific progress is based on theory which, in return, is based on philosophical frameworks. Although the raw information will be available as long as others are succeeding the tradition in a wholesome manner, indeed, they only have that access by extension and will lack the nuance for a fully developed initiation of that knowledge. Moreover, by the fact that the knowledge is accessible by extension, means that the proprietors of the knowledge will be able to command those access points. If there is an input of more theoretical and sociological frameworks within the tradition, the access points will have to endure a philosophical framework to even understand the raw details; a code within a code.

For instance, in the case where medical science was directly linked to philosophical theory, such as the four humors, which is a philosophical perspective of the nature of reality, even if one wanted to access that knowledge base, they could not follow the raw medical details without considering the theory in which it was entrenched.[xix] Thus, it required a philosophical framework of four elements and, more so, of the dynamical nature of reality. It would be fairly difficult to assess a reality framework of such dynamical proportions and use such unethically. The notion goes against the framework of understanding the influences of each aspect of reality, and the nature of any objective has its dynamic counterpart. The medical profession, to be ethically unsound, would need to appropriate that theory to the liminal space of the exacting science without the appropriate introspection of the framework for the rest of their psychological state.

The reason that raw knowledge is accessible secluded from theory is because the original source does not adhere to its traditional basis and thus is also encountering a decline. When raw knowledge continues without an infusion of theory, it will decline, and those who have access by extension will begin to perceive a more raw state of knowledge.

For instance, engineers are a defined category of detailed knowledge without theory; thus, one could not term "engineer" without a preface. We could not have a school of engineers, but only engineers across a spectrum of fields. Thus, academia will always find distaste with engineering schools for their detachment from theory and, thus, their innate decline. The only infusion of vitality is through the fields of engineering to which they enact.

If an individual were an engineer isolated from a field, they would be in wait for a theory to be molded into their applicability through detail. There would be no ethical inquiry because they only exact the theory for its application and serve the details, not the theory. Absolute engineers do not have an ethical compass, as long as they retain the industrial credence of parts that make up a cohesion.

The details do not have any theorized impression but are only working parts of a theory they follow. In fact, the theorizer cannot perform the tedious engineering aspects for fear of losing the theory, as is the case with the seasoned engineer. The engineer finds immediate disassociation when they detach from a field or theory, as they retain the mere understanding of how parts operate in cohesion. Even that simple understanding perpetuates an industrial theory that continues to permeate their worldview. When we remove the industrial theory, even the notion of parts in cohesion is lost.

This is not to cast out the engineer, as they have the keen sensibility of the raw details that are not existentially known to any theorizer, as Aristotle noted of all poetic arts, and which can be extended to all theory, rooted in a certain imagination. They may not have the ability to articulate that sensibility, but there is an intuition to the details that have them follow a sequence that was not considered by theoretical frameworks. [xx]

Moreover, if they follow the sequence of details in that intuitive sense, they may very well notice difficulties in the theory which, of course, they are unable to articulate. For instance, an engineer might notice the specific mold does not offer the intended design, which was already a problem with the theory that attempted to induce a design with materials that do not offer a natural presence and functionality, and in the case of the engineer, a natural transition from mold to part.

When the engineering work is carried out under certain servitude conditions, the resentment of the workers and its political system will also suggest a flaw in the theory as being over-encompassing and disserving functionality.

The engineer will notice these aspects intuitively but will have no way of articulating such complex awareness; to realize the importance of the dynamic between theorizer and engineer. The theorizer will adapt the engineer's intuitive suspicions within their theoretical framework to identify its flaws, while the engineer will have the coveted opportunity of following their industrial work to its theoretical basis. Of course, we would not have them exchange places, but for the engineer to become a theorizer and the theorizer to remain steadfast to the most consistent reality, both will have the final result of being a great asset for society.

Thus, when we encounter something like nuclear power in those who do not share a philosophical framework which is complex and wholesome, we must acknowledge that the internal knowledge is lacking the same thing, to which the notion of having access to nuclear power will fade away. The only case of nuclear demise upon a large scale will be through a transparent choice by the entire communal body. This can be done through political measures, which are representations of the communal body. A mistake can occur, but it is under the guise of a political entity that allows a certain nature to breed a mishap of that scale, which is all represented by the communal body.

When the communal realm declines, so does the cognitive engine that will have the keys to that evolutionary development. There is one juncture that will be threatening to all life forms, and that is a rapid decline of the communal cognitive engine, for there will be a period that will have the access to its advances without any real understanding of its nature. For this reason, there is an evolutionary aspect that will proceed to deliver a decline before the access will be had without reliance on communal choice. Thus, pandemics are not a symptom of communal decline but of *rapid* communal decline.

Before the communal system breaks apart, when there is a sense that such is occurring at too rapid a pace, the evolutionary choice will not allow such speed, for too much access has been meted out, and pandemics are its solution. By using the communal attachment itself, it will propagate its system to deliver dosages of biological decline in order to save the whole form of biological life from rapid decay and its entranceway of annihilation. Moreover, the steady decline has a transition between cultures and/or individuals to retain the most primary information, so that an absolute decline cannot take effect. Similar to the process of human life, which has the steady adulation into elderhood for the transfer of generations. Had the process been through a steep decline or loss of life, there would be no transfer of generations.

The evolutionary choice begins to sacrifice individual organisms in order to preserve the community, but also to degrade the community to such a level that the communal form will be lost and cognitive access will be limited. This will have the effect of losing access to communal cognition, which will also relieve the mind of major evolutionary choice. The evolutionary adaptation of cognitive abilities contains a self-destruct mode, which is embedded by inputting its access through communal attachment, used also to destroy itself by making universal choices of pandemics; destroying cognition through communal sacrifices.

War is another form of evolutionary choice, to have communal bodies test each other into the fallout of a more purified conceptual outlook. Even though war seems like a battle of materiality, the true nature is one of conceptual complexity. The integration of armies at the behest of biological sincerity will assure that even if the weaker defeats the stronger one, they will receive the conceptual buildup of the stronger one just the same. The transfer will take effect, either with the alignment of physicality alongside conceptual complexity, which is usually the case, or with the transfer of conceptual buildup through the totality of warfare.

To maintain even a slight purity to a conceptual tradition, the evolutionary choice is to utilize costly warfare as a method. This method will be noticed even at the individual level, when one feels threatened by a loftier conceptual framework. The sense of threat is not only due to the misinterpretation of the threat as the psyche imagining itself as a physical embodiment, which we have noted in other works, but alternatively, that the evolutionary choice is to find the same level of threat whether biological or conceptual.

In this way, the biological entity will ensure that whatever is more potent as a conceptual framework will be addressed through conflict. Ultimately, the conflict will play out in controversial conversation, carrying the sensibility of warfare without the presence of a biological threat. Nevertheless, it will remain productive. If the conflict were biological, it would not serve the weaker proponent of the conceptual framework, but rather the stronger one, ensuring that its framework is sharp and precise.

Differing from the biological threat, the conceptual one does not concern itself with the self from which it manifests and, in fact, is ready to use its entire organism for the objective. Notice that those who produce biological conflict based on conceptual threats, in which the conceptual threat may have a slight biological effect, are those who are deeply embedded in the communal arena to a point that they are not aware that it is by evolutionary choice and against themselves. From the perspective of the conceptual potency toward the weaker proponent, existing only to propagate a more varying level of framework, there is no need to triumph over that weakness as would be in physical conflict, for it does not contain anything worthwhile and only serves as a backdrop to further their own agenda.

Chapter Six: The Decline of Civilization

The decline of civilization exhibits certain symptoms, which consistently follow a similar pattern. The first arises when representations fail to elicit effective reception, causing them to go unnoticed. This triggers a chain reaction of assumed abundance, or sacrifice of people and product, that does not ascend toward higher consciousness. Those who offer these costs do so believing they will contribute to a higher ordeal, perhaps reflecting back on them so they might move upward along the chain of consciousness. Yet, when their offerings are continuously returned without any reception of their service or product, they are left with a sense of nothingness, caught in a perpetual cycle that leads nowhere.

We term these as representations because they exist solely to serve reflection; like a table full of delicacies that cannot possibly be ingested but are there for alternate purposes. The reflection exists purely for the purpose of consciousness, which must be engaged from a conceptual realm. This requires the attendees to be properly ordered with attention. Deviation may occur when one is at the table without the capacity to reflect at that level, having arrived there through other means.

Surely, such individuals will lose their engagement, as they will be unable to find a reason for their presence. Yet, in the meantime, they will sit at the table, assuming they are adequately partaking in it. Abundance is receptive even to limited consciousness, as it can provide a glimpse of exposure that higher organisms are capable of following. This becomes a strong justification for assuming the engagement is complete, as the experience itself appears to confirm that one is following a chain of consciousness. This is partly true, because the glimpse itself constitutes growth in consciousness. However, without conceptual interaction with the glimpse, it will only be layered upon personhood. The glimpse remains within the realm of consciousness, as it lacks the intellectual attachment to anchor it. Furthermore, it cannot be interacted with and is forced onto selfhood in various forms, which cannot be dismissed when proven harmful to personhood.

That glimpse is meant to be a promise of future receptivity. This becomes problematic for those with little prior consciousness, as they are unable to return the glimpse with an improved sense, since they do not stand above it. Being anchored solely to the experience, without a grander scheme of mental behavior, they are unable to proceed with generative development. The perpetual cycle may continue for a limited period, until it becomes quite clear that one is only participating in the transcendent experience for its sense of vitality, without the use of that vitality. It becomes like the sacrifice of life without the utilization of it. When the psyche becomes aware of this, the promise of future life is seen as a failed endeavor, and even the glimpse begins to fade in vitality.

When those purposes are never fulfilled, all participants in such reflection will no longer be renewed in their purposes, left devoid of any fulfillment at all. The final symptom will be high strains of consciousness that are no longer in participation with those who contributed to their emergence.

Another symptom of decline is the "homebody," marked by the neglect of dynamic receptivity within the home. These are deliberate repressions of the details that reflect the through line of consciousness permeating the homebody. Such individuals will be perceived with resentment, which causes them to carry their own resentment in response to such treatment. The needs of certain members will be neglected due to the absence of a permeating consciousness that supports the humanistic lineage; from conception through personal development. Just as abundance goes unnoticed, within the familial structure, the voices of reprieve, voicing the unsettled experience of not receiving the promised lot, will become a source of resentment.

A third symptom of decline lies in the manner of interaction with children and the elderly. Children represent the wholesome emptiness presumed to be the progress of the adult generation. The elderly, on the other hand, become a source of discomfort, as they represent a previous period that has been neglected by the current generation in favor of fitting their volatile consciousness, unrestricted by the limitations of their lineage.

A fourth symptom is the general decline of memory, whether personal or public. Memory poses a threat to the inconsistencies that current consciousness attempts to conceal. Memory is the lineage of consciousness, always containing the question of logical consistency throughout its progression to the present.

A fifth symptom is the fading reverence toward parents, not for specific, contextual reasons, but because they claim a lineage to the current mindset and existence. In this sense, parents become a memory of consciousness, which is presumed unnecessary for continued existence.

Further Reading

Arendt, Hannah. *The Human Condition.* Chicago: University of Chicago Press, 1958.

Aristotle. *Poetics.* Translated by M. Heath. New York: Penguin Classics, 1996. (Original work ca. 335 BCE)

Aristotle. *Politics.* Translated by Benjamin Jowett. In *The Basic Works of Aristotle*, edited by Richard McKeon, 1127–1316. New York: Random House, 1941.

Bernardi, Daniel. *Narrative Landmines.* New Brunswick, NJ: Rutgers University Press, 2012.

Freud, Sigmund. *Civilization and Its Discontents.* Translated by James Strachey. New York: W. W. Norton & Company, 1961.

Hippocrates. *On the Nature of Man.* Translated by W. H. S. Jones. Loeb Classical Library. Cambridge, MA: Harvard University Press, 1923. (Original work ca. 400 BCE)

Kessler, Karl A. *The Art of Creation.* New York: Harcourt, Brace and Company, 1923.

Lévi-Strauss, Claude. *Tristes Tropiques.* Translated by John Russell. New York: Criterion Books, 1961. (Original work 1955)

MacAskill, William. *Doing Good Better: How Effective Altruism Can Help You Make a Difference.* New York: Avery, 2015.

Marmot, M. G., S. Stansfeld, C. Patel, F. North, J. Head, I. White, E. Brunner, A. Feeney, and G. D. Smith. "Health

Inequalities among British Civil Servants: The Whitehall II Study." *The Lancet* 337, no. 8754 (1991): 1387–1393.

Nelson, Hilde Lindemann. *Damaged Identities, Narrative Repair.* Ithaca, NY: Cornell University Press, 2001.

Perry, Stephen. "Hart on Social Rules and the Foundations of Law: Liberating the Internal Point of View." *Fordham Law Review* 75, no. 3 (2006): 1171–1239.

Plato. *Meno.* Translated by G. M. A. Grube. In *Plato: Complete Works*, edited by J. M. Cooper, 870–897. Indianapolis, IN: Hackett, 1981.

Shakespeare, William. *Hamlet.* Edited by Harold Jenkins. London: Methuen, 1982.

Smith, Anthony D. *The Ethnic Origins of Nations.* Oxford: Blackwell, 1996.

Suetonius. *The Twelve Caesars.* Translated by Robert Graves. London: Penguin Classics, 1957. (esp. Nero, section 28)

<u>Notes</u>

---

[i] Kessler, Karl A. The Art of Creation. New York: Harcourt, Brace and Company, 1923.

[ii] Aristotle. Politics. Translated by Benjamin Jowett. In The Basic Works of Aristotle, edited by Richard McKeon, 1127–1316. New York: Random House, 1941.

[iii] This disparity might be noticed by students with complex reception.

[iv] Marmot, M. G., Stansfeld, S., Patel, C., North, F., Head, J., White, I., Brunner, E., Feeney, A., & Smith, G. D. (1991). Health inequalities among British civil servants: The Whitehall II study. The Lancet, 337(8754), 1387–1393.

[v] Stephen Perry, Hart on Social Rules and the Foundations of Law: Liberating the Internal Point of View, 75 Fordham L. Rev. 1171 (2006).

[vi] Perry, Stephen. "Hart on Social Rules and the Foundations of Law: Liberating the Internal Point of View." Fordham Law Review 75, no. 3 (2006): 1171–1239.

[vii] Arendt, Hannah. The Human Condition. Chicago: University of Chicago Press, 1958.

[viii] MacAskill, William. Doing Good Better: How Effective Altruism Can Help You Make a Difference. New York: Avery, 2015.

[ix] Lévi-Strauss, Claude. Tristes Tropiques. Translated by John Russell. New York: Criterion Books,

[x] Freud, Sigmund. Civilization and Its Discontents. Translated by James Strachey. New York: W. W. Norton & Company, 1961.

[xi] 1961Smith, Anthony D. The Ethnic Origins of Nations. Oxford: Blackwell, 1996.

[xii] Suetonius, The Twelve Caesars (esp. Nero, section 28).

[xiii] Plato. (1981). Meno (G. M. A. Grube, Trans.). In J. M. Cooper (Ed.), Plato: Complete works (pp. 870–897). Indianapolis, IN: Hackett.

[xiv] Shakespeare, William. Hamlet. Edited by Harold Jenkins. London: Methuen, 1982.

[xv] Bostrom, Nick. "Existential Risks: Analyzing Human Extinction Scenarios and Related Hazards." Journal of Evolution and Technology 9, no. 1 (2002).

[xvi] Bostrom, Nick. "Existential Risks: Analyzing Human Extinction Scenarios and Related Hazards." Journal of Evolution and Technology 9, no. 1 (2002).

[xvii] Bernardi, Daniel. Narrative Landmines. New Brunswick, NJ: Rutgers University Press, 2012.

[xviii] Nelson, Hilde Lindemann. Damaged Identities, Narrative Repair. Ithaca, NY: Cornell University Press, 2001.

[xix] Hippocrates. (1923). On the Nature of Man (W. H. S. Jones, Trans.). Loeb Classical Library. Cambridge, MA: Harvard University Press. (Original work ca. 400 BCE)

[xx] Aristotle. (1996). Poetics (M. Heath, Trans.). New York, NY: Penguin Classics. (Original work ca. 335 BCE)